The Black Body

For a complete list of titles in the Other Voices of Italy series, please see the last page of the book.

OVOI

Other Voices of Italy

Editors: Alessandro Vettori, Sandra Waters, and Eilis Kierans

This series presents texts in a variety of genres originally written in Italian. Much like the symbiotic relationship between the wolf and the raven, its principal aim is to introduce new or past authors—who have until now been marginalized—to an English-speaking readership. This series also highlights contemporary transnational authors, as well as writers who have never been translated or who are in need of a fresh or contemporary translation. The series further aims to increase the appreciation of translation as an art form that enhances the importance of cultural diversity.

This book was written by a Black Italian woman whose experiences of deep-seated racism and misogyny reflect a problematic (at best) contemporary Italy. Even though she was born in Rome, she is not accepted as a "true" Italian because of the color of her skin and must adhere to the severely outdated law that forces her to go to the immigration office to submit her fingerprints every year. Regardless of the societal and bureaucratic hoops that she is forced to jump through, she thrives as a singer, dancer, rapper, and producer. She embraces her African roots and learns much about herself and her family when she takes a soul-searching trip to Liberia, her parents' home country. Anna Maria Gehnyei—known artistically as Karima 2G—lives suspended between two cultures, all the while keeping both of them nestled in her heart.

The Black Body

ANNA MARIA GEHNYEI

Translated by Eilis Kierans and Sandra Waters

Foreword by Igiaba Scego

Rutgers University Press
New Brunswick, Camden, and Newark, New Jersey
London and Oxford, UK

Rutgers University Press is a department of Rutgers, The State University of New Jersey, one of the leading public research universities in the nation. By publishing worldwide, it furthers the University's mission of dedication to excellence in teaching, scholarship, research, and clinical care.

Library of Congress Cataloging-in-Publication Data
Names: Gehnyei, Anna Maria, author. | Waters, Sandra, translator. | Kierans, Eilis, translator. | Scego, Igiaba, writer of foreword.
Title: The black body / Anna Maria Gehnyei; translated by Eilis Kierans and Sandra Waters; foreword by Igiaba Scego.
Other titles: Corpo nero. English
Description: New Brunswick: Rutgers University Press, 2025. | Series: Other voices of Italy | Includes bibliographical references.
Identifiers: LCCN 2024058540 | ISBN 9781978840973 (paperback) | ISBN 9781978840980 (hardcover) | ISBN 9781978840997 (epub)
Subjects: LCSH: Gehnyei, Anna Maria. | Women singers—Italy—Biography. | Women, Black—Italy—Biography. | Children of immigrants—Italy—Biography. | Children, Kpelle—Italy—Biography. | Women, Black—Italy—Social conditions. | Girls, Black—Italy—Social conditions. | LCGFT: Autobiographies.
Classification: LCC ML420.G324 A3 2025 | DDC 782.42164092 [B]—dc23/eng/20241206
LC record available at https://lccn.loc.gov/2024058540

A British Cataloging-in-Publication record for this book is available from the British Library.

∞ The paper used in this publication meets the requirements of the American National Standard for Information Sciences—Permanence of Paper for Printed Library Materials, ANSI Z39.48-1992.

rutgersuniversitypress.org

I dedicate this first fruit to my ancestors and
to my entire family tree.

My body moves and speaks without taboos.

Contents

Foreword

Literary Writing in the Words of Anna Maria Gehnyei

While reading the pages of *The Black Body* by Anna Maria Gehnyei, also known as Karima 2G, you get the sense that the book is written by many hands: the hands of Anna, the person holding the pen, along with the hands of her family and ancestors. Her writing is authorial, yet it is never the work of just one individual. Echoing the rich traditions of African and Afro-descendant literature, her words draw upon a collective consciousness spanning centuries.

Anna Maria Gehnyei is a multifaceted artist: she writes, sings, dances, creates. She fought hard, like every Black person, to be embraced by this word: artist. In fact, creativity—art—is often denied Black people. Instead, their contributions are dismissed as mere testimony and treated primarily as personal accounts. But by rendering her experience a universal one, Anna Maria Gehnyei follows in the footsteps of fellow writers from across the pond, from Toni Morrison to Alice Walker. It can be said that Anna *escrivive* ("writes-lives"), a word that derives from the Portuguese *escrevivência*. This concept was crafted by the Afro-Brazilian author Conceição

Evaristo to explain the tightknit intertwining, like a cross-stitch of stories, between the lived experience and creativity of the Black artist. You live, you write, you escrivive. And this is precisely what Anna Maria Gehnyei does over and over again on every page: she weaves together profound and nuanced plotlines.

In the Italian panorama where this book has landed, Gehnyei may undoubtedly be one of the most interesting voices because she navigates various territories without being confined by any one of them. *The Black Body* can be defined as a Creole, diasporic, migrant, and hybrid text. But if we must find a word to describe this book, it is the word freedom. In her work, Gehnyei celebrates the freedom of writing as an essential ingredient for a life lived authentically. The story is told succinctly: Anna Maria Gehnyei sheds light on her Black body, and on the Black body of her family, from Liberia to Italy. She recounts the decision (a pivotal moment in fate) of a Kpelle man to leave Liberia. A man who—very attached to tradition—asks the village leaders for their approval before taking a step toward the future. The book's form resembles a diary that is, not by chance, reminiscent of *Forbidden Notebook* by Alba de Céspedes, a book that details the ebbs and flows of the protagonist's heart. But if the protagonist of *Forbidden Notebook* is always on the verge of a nervous breakdown, Gehnyei's writing, on the other hand, has a healing quality about it. Each word, even in the most painful and introspective passages, is never devoid of hope. In the end, there is forever a sun that rises or even a lesson to be learned from evil. Perhaps Anna Maria Gehnyei drew this technique from music. She needs only a few brush strokes, as if they were harmonious notes, to give color to the page. The color is that of her skin, but it is also the color of the Liberian food that her large family cherishes around the table, or the color of a Roman sky beaming with light that shoots through the clouds in a state of absolute perfection. The words are simple, and you can see how much the author has worked toward subtraction, of whittling down her ideas to the essential and erasing superfluous words. At its core, this book seeks to understand the author's divided identity—Liberian and Italian—and how these seemingly conflicting aspects ultimately converge into a single, unified self. Gehnyei arrives at her destination without making useless detours. And each page is carved out like the verse of a song. No doubt the influence of musical lyrics, which incorporate rhythm, sound, and brevity, is deeply felt. After all, Alfred Hitchcock also said the following about his characters: everything must be credible; they must be credible in everything they do. If I put a doctor on stage, Hitchcock remarked, regarding James Stewart's role in *The Man Who Knew Too Much*, I must make him a doctor until the very end. And here Stewart, before giving Doris Day the news of her son's kidnapping, gives her sleeping pills and calms her down because he knows what's coming—an incurable, suffocating pain. And Anna Maria Gehnyei applies this rule to both the authorial self and the character self. And then she gives the reader the feeling that what we are reading isn't something born in an instant, in months of writing, but a text that speaks to us from far away, a geographical and temporal distance—a text that speaks of yesterday, the day before yesterday, of the unfathomable time of her ancestors, and where the past and future are intimately linked. It is a book that comes looking for its author. It is the book that everyone in her house knew she would, soon enough, one day write. So, Anna Maria Gehnyei has a mission because it is not only her story and the story of her family, but it is also the story of a community of walkers and dreamers.

It is already clear from these few lines of commentary that reading Gehnyei's *The Black Body* is a journey, if even just the beginning of one, because it takes us into a dimension of the story that is dreamlike and necessary—a dimension that is nourished by her mother's African stories, by her father's Afrobeat music. They are what brings her closer to Liberia, the land of free men, the country to which many African Americans have returned after generations of slavery. But then there is a Blackness in reading the book that we cannot take for granted, a Blackness that the author discovers piece by piece. She who was also educated to respect white people by her parents discovers that her body is not respected in return. And she will have to decolonize an idea that was instilled in her and find weapons with which to defend herself from a world where systemic racism is still hegemonic, where the racist buzz does not stop suffocating us.

The most painful pages of the book are about racism. The author is mocked, insulted, and humiliated. In fact, she is forced to navigate that uncertain territory of fear, that fear of losing the body that Ta Nehisi Coates discusses and that unites many Black men and women. Circumstances require Anna Maria Gehnyei to be perpetually on guard and alert. And this exhausts her, destroys her body. But Gehnyei, fortunately, never gives up. And this is where *The Black Body* is healing. It teaches you to stand up for yourself despite everything. It's healing for those who write but also for those who read. It's a book that, once closed, leaves us a legacy of tenacity and courage but also an immense desire to find a new language—a language of rights, struggle, and full awareness of oneself, through which we can be truly free. *The Black Body* is a book with many souls, but it is also a book that talks about Rome, or rather North Rome, a part of the capital city frequented by rich people, a part of the city without mercy. In this description of North Rome, the author doesn't place herself outside the context of the city. She knows she is part of the Roman-ness she describes. The streets of Rome are also hers, especially hers. And it is in this urban context that she encounters fascism, ignorance, and racism. When you are the only Black person in the city, neighborhood, school, or room, encounters with racism are inevitable. She sees the face of a teacher, of a group of bullies, of a boy she may like, but they are on the other side of the fence. Racism seems to nest everywhere, even in Black people themselves. But Gehnyei faces it without ever hiding. *The Black Body* makes us understand that it's not only in lived experience that we fight against this disease, but we also do it through our own artistic tools and cultural militancy. Art is the answer because it helps her to never lose sight of the nuances. The author does not like to generalize, despite having lived and suffered through these experiences. She examines all her experiences with a critical and compassionate eye, making the page itself a splendid example of an anti-racist vaccine.

For Anna Maria Gehnyei, words save, form, create, and embrace. Not by chance, space and time are modeled on the noise of dreams. Liberation comes only through a careful elaboration of who one has been, is, and wants to be, as when the author goes to Liberia. Only when she visits Africa does she understand that Europe is also partly her home. Gehnyei is in fact not only Italian or only Liberian. She is a Black Italian, an Afro-European, an Afropean, an Italian Liberian, and a Liberian Italian, but first of all, she is herself: a free artist—an "I" that through writing transforms into a "we."

The book also holds a place in the world of publishing that cannot be underestimated. In the Italian landscape, Black people struggle to publish and when they do, they are crushed by a marketing strategy that distorts them. Anna Maria Gehnyei has traversed the Italian publishing jungle unscathed and additionally has succeeded in imposing her authorial voice. Hers is a voice that does not want to be harnessed (which happened somewhat to her parents in Italy) but that wants to be free to be itself, always. For this reason, it is important to say that the book is not only its content but also its style, tone, rhythm, and vision. It's a text that brings Italian literature into the contemporary world, and without any kind of rhetoric—the book is not a book of denunciation nor that of a victim. It brings the level of literary exchange to a high, necessary level. It's a pearl of a book that will help many people of African descent to pick up a pen and begin to exist on the page. It's a beautiful book, one that we will talk about for a long time.

Igiaba Scego

Translator's Note

Translating Anna Maria Gehnyei's *Il corpo nero* (2023) has been a profound journey of learning and empathy. As white women, we have been privileged to remain untouched by the racism and discrimination Gehnyei endured at the hands of educators, peers, and law enforcement. However, through the powerful and deeply personal act of translation, we have gained poignant insight into the often harsh and unforgiving reality Gehnyei continues to face on a regular basis. Indeed, the relationship between translation and empathy is profound and multifaceted. In translating Gehnyei's words from one language to another, we dug deeply into the cultural context of the source text to connect more intimately to the author's experience and perspective. In turn, the emotional resonance we experienced with the words of Gehnyei allowed us to better capture the tone, syntax, and register of her text, components that vary widely throughout the book.

The opening chapter of her autobiographical account, titled "Seven Years Old," depicts Anna and her twin sister as frustrated schoolchildren. In the distracted first-person storytelling style of a child, Anna recounts the discrimination they experience on the playground through the eyes of innocent yet mischievous little girls. She expresses herself in simple, straightforward language, "My backpack is so bulky that it makes me slow as a snail. And I already know that as soon as I'm on the bus, I'll be subjected to those strange stares that make me want to hide my face" (1). In essence, the tone of the opening chapter is playful, curious, and frank while the register is informal and conversational.

As Anna matures into a young woman, the text becomes increasingly sophisticated. In the chapter titled "Fingerprints," she is not yet an Italian citizen and thus is required to have her fingerprints taken at police headquarters. She expresses, "It takes a little over an hour to arrive and, as soon as I get off the bus, I see that there are already more than one hundred people in a long line that snakes down Via Teofilo Patini. I slink through the barriers and find myself among immigrants, migrants, asylum seekers, embassy officials, and second-generation kids like me who feel out of place in this mix of humanity" (104). No longer a child, Anna's sentences are both short and punchy as well as long and rhythmic. Although the register is undeniably higher here, the tone is nonetheless informal and conversational.

As the narrative unfolds, Anna's physical and emotional growth is laced with sarcasm and humor. Indubitably, humor is a coping mechanism that provides Anna and her community relief. Humor offers an outlet for their struggles and helps them process painful experiences. In the chapter "Oceanic Currents," friends and family members are attending Uncle Isacco's funeral in Sicily when policemen arrive and start checking their documents. A policeman turns to a young woman holding a newborn and asks her how she got there. Anna translates the policeman's words for the girl. "'By boat,' was her response, with the 'b' so stressed that it resounded throughout that tense silence. A light wind swept across the funeral and we all started to laugh in unison, like Uncle Isacco would have done. He liked to laugh and he would have appreciated this girl's unintentional joke" (138). In essence, humor provides a healthy means of expression for people dealing with discomfort and oppression, transforming silence and suffering into a shared experience that fosters community and resilience.

As Anna continues to mature and prepares to connect with her roots in Liberia, her prose is often poetic and relies on precise sound, rhythm, and cadence. Indeed, capturing these elements in translation while maintaining the source text was a delicate dance. For example, in the chapter "I Dream of Water," Anna dreams that she is submerged beneath water, struggling to subvert her fear and stay afloat. She conveys, "I am lying on the bed, my anguish has faded and I relish the fresh morning air that drifts through the open window. The curtain ebbs and flows like a sail and it reminds me of the movements of the water, the waves of the sea into which I dive warily, while keeping one eye on land to make sure I don't go too far" (117). In this passage, we sought to bring poetic justice to the source text by echoing the cadence of the waves through the rhythm and syntax of the sentence. In essence, we have craftily preserved or, in some instances, relied on compensation to elevate the language and aesthetics of the English rendering.

In essence, we have set out to provide you with a modest taste of the rich and varied chapters you will encounter in Gehnyei's autobiographical work. Undoubtedly, each chapter is a poignant fragment of the author's life, tiny pieces that she has intricately woven together to make sense of her complex Liberian-Italian identity. As translators, working on this project was a true labor of love that has nurtured greater cultural sensitivity and awareness on our part. We have rigorously edited and reworked the text to bring it closer and closer to the author's lived experience. We humbly hope to have been faithful to the author's experience.

Eilis Kierans and Sandra Waters

The Black Body

1
Seven Years Old

I have to climb three steep steps to board the yellow school bus that picks us up at our doorstep each morning. Those steps are too big for a seven-year-old girl like me. My sister Maria and I are the same height, but she is faster than I am. My backpack is so bulky that it makes me slow as a snail. And I already know that as soon as I'm on the bus, I'll be subjected to those strange stares that make me want to hide my face.

Without making eye contact with a single soul, I sit next to Maria on those faded red seats spewing yellow foam.

The stop-and-go of the bus makes my body move back and forth, and I cling to the seat in front of me to keep my balance. My Black hands brush the blonde hair of the little girl seated in front of me. Her ponytail swishes smoothly from side to side while our braids sway stiffly.

The journey is short and we quickly arrive at our school, Giustiniana. I try my best to line up and get off the bus, but not one kid will let me through. Meanwhile, my sister nudges me as if it were my fault that I can't get out.

It's finally my turn and once again I carefully descend the stairs.

I watch my feet climb down one after another. My shoes are red and Maria's shoes are blue. It's the only detail that sets us apart these days, besides the elastics in our braids; mine are green and hers are blue. Mom always dresses us in the same outfits, as if it weren't enough that we are the spitting image of each other. She tells us that we're beautiful, that we're unique.

But to others, we are just the Black twins.

Finally off the bus, we have to weave through a sea of cars parked on the sidewalk and make room for parents accompanying their children to school. The street is narrow and many students attend Giustiniana. They are all white kids.

I head to the school gate, take a quick look at the playground, my favorite place, and then I walk to the main entrance. The school is painted pink on the outside. The hall inside is lined with classroom doors, including mine or rather *ours*, because me and Maria are together. I like going to class, especially when it's cold outside, because the classroom is always warm and its green-colored walls are cheerful. The wall is dotted with many wooden coat hooks, but I don't know why I can never find a place for my jacket and I always have to put mine over Maria's.

The class has twenty students in it, but we have a big classroom so we are comfortable. We often switch seats so we can get to know each other better, but I'm shy and I barely talk to anyone. Today I'm seated at a desk near the window. While the teacher is explaining something, I get distracted and watch the little birds resting outside on the branches of a tree sprouting small green leaves.

A clock hangs on the wall above the chalkboard behind the teacher. I look at it repeatedly in anticipation of recess time. When the bell finally rings and it's snack time, the teacher takes us outside because it's a beautiful day and spring is in bloom. We only have one rule outside in the yard, besides not hurting each other: don't go to the other side of the building and stay in the yard.

Maria and I begin to run like our classmates who are playing tag—but nobody chases us and we almost stop playing as soon as we start. Then we decide to join a group of students from another class who are playing hide-and-seek.

"Can we play with you?" Maria asks a little girl our age.

I hide behind my sister while the girl talks it over with two others. I realize they are laughing into their hands. They respond yes. Maria lets out a squeal of joy, but it seems strange to me that they accepted us so quickly. In fact, nobody came looking for us when we hid, and the game ended and began again without us as if their plan were to leave us in hiding.

Maria is not afraid to confront them and protest.

"Why didn't anyone come find us?"

"Because you're Black," one of them says, as if she already had her answer ready.

"And what does that have to do with anything?" she replies, looking her straight in the eyes.

"We don't want to play with you," another girl answers, while a boy next to her curls his lip at us in contempt.

Maria and I distance ourselves, and I want to tell the teachers. But then I see them sitting and chatting among themselves, and I already know that they'll say the same ol' thing they do every other time: we can play among ourselves, there are two of us—and then nobody will bother us.

Without a word, and with one quick look, we set out to do something absolutely forbidden: we make our way toward the back of the school where the gym is located.

The door is open and nobody is inside. First we look around a little, and then we grab a rope and begin to jump, tripping and laughing because we aren't very good. Then we hop up on the trampolines. We grab a ball and manage to throw it back and forth over the volleyball net, which isn't very high. We try to do cartwheels and collapse on the bouncy blue trampolines.

We are all alone in that enormous space just for us. I'm happy and I know Maria is too.

At some point, we both set our sights on a staircase that leads to the rooftop above the gym. Without giving it another thought, we agree to check it out. From high up, everything is even more picturesque. We see the other children in the distance and they look like tiny ants. We also see some people approaching—the teachers. We hear them calling our names, and then they spot us looming up above, all by ourselves.

I'm afraid of being yelled at but I don't want to get down. I want to stay here with Maria so that nobody forgets to find us or makes fun of us because we are Black.

"Anna! Maria! Be careful. You can't stay up there. Go to the top of the stairs. I'm coming to get you so we can climb down together," one of the teachers says, shouting but without sounding angry.

In the meantime, some of our classmates arrive. Maybe the teachers yelled at them because they begin to bellow: "Come down and play with us!"

A teacher comes to help us down, and some classmates immediately start to hug us. I still want to be alone with my sister, but I think how wonderful it would be to hang out with all the other kids, how wonderful it would be if the fact that we are Black didn't matter to them at all.

2
African Braids

"Ambarabà, ciccì, coccò"[1]

As soon as Maria starts the rhyme, slowly and lacking oomph, I interrupt her.

"Look, it's useless even if I lose. I don't wanna go first this week. I started last Sunday. It's your turn!"

"It's not true. Last time I went first. It's your turn to start!

We could easily go back and forth like this for an hour, but Mom gets in the middle and tells us not to fight, that it isn't a big deal who goes first because in the end, she is going to give us *both* braids.

Today is Sunday and, like every Sunday, today is dedicated to doing hair. Mom says it's the same way in Africa. In Liberia, every Sunday morning all the little girls get their hair done in anticipation of church and then school.

[1] "Ambarabà, ciccì, coccò" is used similarly to "eeny, meeny, miny, moe." It is a nursery rhyme that is often used to settle an argument or to select a person to complete a particular task, often in the context of children's games.

Maria starts to play "eeny, meeny, miny, moe" again and I'm happy because in the end I win. I bought myself some more time before I have to sit still for an hour while Mom tries to loosen all the knots in my hair so she can comb through it. Maria gets a little angry, but she knows it's useless, so she begins to undo her braids from last Sunday. I, on the other hand, begin to gingerly hop and sing but not too much.

Mom stops me right away: "Anna, you also need to undo your braids since you always take so long." Meanwhile, she gathers the creams she will slather all over our scalps. They smell so good, especially the coconut one, which I'm tempted to eat. But I'm already nine years old, and I know the difference between food and hair products.

Mom places the big jar of coconut cream on the table, which is still smaller than the tub of olive oil cream. Next to it she places the green jars of lanolin cream and Dax Pomade infused with vegetable oil. The pomade makes my hair shiny, and we go all the way to a tiny store near Termini Station just to buy it. Mom rides the bus there and sometimes she takes us with her.

Next to all of her products, Mom prepares the brushes and combs. She takes one of them into the kitchen—the hot comb. It's made of metal and needs to be heated over the stove for a while so that it can smooth out afro hair like ours. But I'm scared of that thing because it burns, and I'm worried that Mom will mistakenly brush my ears or head. One time she grazed my ear and I still remember the pain perfectly well. Mom, however, says that it's the only way to loosen the knots in our hair and to make them soft. But by the time she's done, my head hurts. To my dismay, it's time for me to take the comb with the thin tip and undo my braids.

Meanwhile, seated in my usual seat at the dinner table, I open a book and read, turning pages as I loosen my braids. When Mom sees me, she gets mad because she says I'm slow on purpose. Maria is already done and can go wash her hair while I still have half of my braids to undo.

I close my book, but I get lost in thought and it takes me a while, also because I have to be careful not to tear my hair out. When I'm done, it's my turn to wash my tresses in the bathroom sink, with Mom's help. She tries to be careful, but the water continues to stream down my face, and I can't stand when the soap gets in my eyes, or even worse, runs down my neck and then my back.

While Mom washes my hair, she asks me what kind of hairdo I want because every week she does something different. We can choose between long braids, called African braids, or very tight braids that pull a bit, called cornrows. But Mom makes intricate designs all over our heads and I think they are very pretty. Sometimes she gives us a high braid, a type of ponytail, instead. I don't like this hairstyle as much but it's quicker to do.

"No, I don't want cornrows today. It takes too much time!"

Maria is already done, but I don't want to stay still for more than an hour, even if in the end I will have those pretty waves that zigzag along my head a little and then hang, like normal braids, down my neck.

"Mom, today I can't get braids in my hair because my head already hurts a bit." I try again, but she doesn't fall for it.

"That's enough, Anna. You think any excuse is a good one! I don't really believe that you have a headache."

At that point, I dare not open my mouth. She sits in the armchair and I am between her legs.

I try not to complain anymore because today is also Dad's day off. He's in the room with us and I don't want to cause a lot of chaos. He wants to listen to music, so he sits close to the stereo and begins to play his songs. As he puffs on a cigarette, he tells me that if I focus on the notes of the music, I'll feel less pain when Mom tries to untangle my hair.

As Dad's tunes fill the room, he turns on the heater so we don't get too cold. We only use the heater on Sundays because Dad says that gas tanks are very expensive. Understandably, our house is always cold during the winter.

Mom begins to apply cream to my hair. The sweet scent of coconut makes me feel better. Before adding in another cream, she combs my hair with the afro comb, a metal tool with a fist-shaped handle that makes my hair really soft.

I think of my schoolmates who have those lovely long locks that are so straight and easy to brush. They don't have to spend hours every Sunday getting their braids done; they are free to play whatever they want. And while I ruminate, Mom gets up and heads to the kitchen to get the hot comb, which she has heated over the stove. When she returns, she runs it through the tips of my hair very slowly and carefully. The comb really burns, so to avoid burning my ears, Mom covers them with a towel.

She always tells me that in order to be a lovely little girl, I have to suffer a bit. But she knows I'm scared that she'll burn me. To distract me, she gives me my favorite doll Molly, the only Black doll I have, so I can rock her. Other times, she puts on cartoons, but only if Dad isn't listening to music.

After she gets out all the knots, she starts to braid my hair. She is very nimble, and her hands move back and forth, right to left, and it feels like they are flying over my head. When she finishes a braid, she puts a tiny elastic band at the end so that it doesn't come undone. Or sometimes she uses a hair clip or one of the many colorful beads we have.

When all the braids are finished, I run to the bathroom to look at myself in the mirror, because even if I don't like spending a lot of time getting my hair done on Sunday mornings, I'm proud to go to school with a new hairdo every Monday.

3
Snakes and Dad

After school I spend time with my friends. I'm only friends with the kids who live in my building or close to us. The little buildings where we live are all connected; I'm in number five, my friend Galisa lives in number three, and my cousin Moses is in number four. Moses is the only cousin I know. His parents, Uncle Samba and Auntie Alice, are from Sierra Leone and are my parents' best friends. And even if our parents aren't really related, it's like Moses really is my cousin. And then there's Jonathan, who lives in building number six; he's the son of an Italian woman and an American man, and Andrea and Luca, who are two brothers who are a little older than me and the others. Me and Maria play with them in the yard when it's not raining.

We really like the swings, even if it's a bit boring to have to wait our turn. The worst is when Jonathan swings, because he never wants to get off and we have to ask him many times before he decides it's our turn. Sometimes I get tired of waiting so I pick up the ball and call the others to go play on the volleyball court. There's a net there too, but it's a bit old and torn, and above all it's very high and it's hard to get the ball over it.

Boys don't really like volleyball and sometimes they don't even answer me if I ask them to play. Then it's only us girls to make a few serves to one another or, if we remember to bring the jump rope, we have fun with that and challenge each other to see who can jump the longest.

In the spring, the yard fills up with daisies, and me and Maria always pick some to bring to our mom who puts them in a glass and keeps them on the cabinet next to the TV until they wilt and get thrown away. Luca, Andrea, and Jonathan never want to pick flowers with us—only Moses every now and again. They like to catch bugs or pull the tails off lizards. When they succeed, they always laugh like crazy to see that piece of tail move by itself while what remains of the lizard tries to wiggle away.

Where the yard ends, there is a grove and when we all go down to the courtyard in the summer evenings because it's too hot inside, we see lots of moving luminous dots among the trees. Andrea said that they're called fireflies, but to me they look like a magical swarm of flying lights.

Today is pretty chilly even though it's spring and me and Maria, together with the others, have decided not to stay in the garden but to go to the lawn behind the apartment buildings because there's more sun there. Mom doesn't like it when we go there because she always says that we don't know what could be in the grass, especially when it's tall like now.

We move among the tall green blades that shift as we pass and then snap back into place. Luca is at the head of the line. We're pretending to be explorers but at a certain point Luca stops and everyone else does too. I'm the last in line and I don't understand what's happening, so I make my way to see what everyone is looking at, so still and silent. Among the blades of grass there's a snake. Andrea shouts that it is a viper and then everyone starts running away and screaming. In a flash, some parents come looking for us, worried. Mom comes too, and as soon as she understands what's happening, leaves immediately, and I know she's not running away but she's going to call Dad.

In the meantime, the doorman, Luigi, has also arrived, who lives in building number one but often wanders around the other buildings to make sure that everything is in order. However, Luigi doesn't go to see for himself; he remains at a distance to talk to the other adults and I hear him complaining that someone should come and cut that grass and everyone agrees with him.

Dad shows up a little later and, without even thinking about it, makes his way to the place we pointed out, looks around a little, and bends down. Then, when he gets up again, he has the viper in his hands.

We are all amazed and frightened, but Dad has an expression that drives away all our worries. With one hand he holds the head of the viper and with the other the tail. The animal shakes all over and it scares me a lot and I hope Papa doesn't let it go otherwise I'll have to start running very fast.

My friends and Maria come closer to get a better look while I stay a step behind. Dad laughs as he calls us a bunch of wimps. Then he stops and adds: "This here is nothing; come to Africa if you want to see what real snakes are like!"

I hear the other kids quietly saying to each other that Dad is a hero and so I pluck up the courage and go up to him to ask how he managed to grab it and if he was at least a little scared, but he walks away without answering me, to set the viper free who knows where. I feel a little upset but my mother explains to me that in Africa, my father grew up with snakes because in his village, Wongbai, there are so many of these creatures and children play with them without getting scared.

Mom doesn't want us to ask Dad about Liberia, especially about Wongbai, because there, boys do things they can't tell girls, not even their sisters, and a dad can't tell his daughters. However, Mom secretly tells us some things, that guys have tests they have to pass and that holding a snake in your hand is a test. When the boys get older, they are taken away from the village to pass tests of courage. I think Dad did too and that's why he has those little circles all over his back. When he gets dressed he is very quick to put on his shirt because he doesn't want us to see his skin, but I almost always manage to catch a glimpse, even if I would like to see more closely and I have so many things to ask him. Sometimes I've tried but he's never answered me; it seems that he doesn't even hear my questions. When I ask him about other things, he always answers me and often explains what I don't understand—but he never talks about Africa.

Dad once overheard Mom telling me about her village. I was a little shaken and I was afraid he'd get angry, but he remained calm and told me that if I want to know more, he'll let me watch a film; in fact we'll all watch it together. The film is called *Roots.* You can't be Black if you haven't seen *Roots* first, said Dad.

4
Scars on Skin

If I could write a letter to my father, I would tell him all that I've kept inside until today, and I would ask him questions that I've never been able to ask because I'm not supposed to know certain things.

If I could, I'd say that his severity has always frightened me, but above all it's kept me at a distance. Those scars on his skin, perfectly drawn furrows on which I have never been able to place my finger as a child; they are the mystery that I am not allowed to know.

Dad, I would say, your gaze blocks me and your silence is a wall between us. It was a wall that you built so that I couldn't even look at that body of yours, sculpted like the statue of a hero disfigured by who knows what practice of his village.

Men have secrets that women are not supposed to know. One cannot disrespect tradition.

Dad, I know that your composure comes from such a place. Something happened to your body that also marked scars on your soul and you keep it all inside and you have never acknowledged it.

Those marks are wounds that will never heal even if you thought there was a medicine for doing so.

You thought that it would all go away, that medicine could be the consolation that you were looking for all of your life—yet you never found it anywhere. I watched you drink that medicine and every sip was a relief for you and you didn't realize that it was as cold and common as the bottle that contained it. Sometimes I would have liked to have a few sips too, to try to understand what you felt when you withdrew with it.

We were all in the same room but it was like you were alone.

Do you remember that one time I even asked you if I could taste it? You answered me with such a sharp no that I never had the courage to ask you again. Your response made me understand that your relationship with that amber liquid was not healthy. And I don't know if you told me no to protect me or because you didn't want someone to share these moments of yours. What I do know, however, is that I was jealous.

If it hadn't been for the medicine, perhaps, you would have told me how you felt when you lost your job at the embassy and then found yourself doing manual labor, almost like a slave.

It was Mom who told me how things went.

I knew that you studied in Monrovia, in the capital, and that you met each other and fell in love there. I also knew that to support yourself, you worked for a company that built roads and that the person who would later become the Liberian ambassador in Italy wanted you with him in Rome. What I didn't know is that after a few years, with the conflicts in Liberia growing ever more intense, the ambassador no longer felt safe even in Italy and decided to flee to America in the dead of night.

You found yourselves alone, without jobs, in a foreign country. You lived in a villa that wasn't yours but you stayed there for a while. Then Mom started working as a cleaning lady and you as a bricklayer.

Mom also told me that both of you really wanted to go back to Liberia and build a future there, but then my sister and I arrived and our birth upset all these plans.

I know you're stuck in a country that's not yours, but you don't have to feel alone. I'm with you.

I remember every year at Christmas when I was little I would write my little letter to Santa Claus.

I knew that the small man was too white for you to believe in him, but I hoped you would read my words and the requests I made. But I would write in Italian and then one year I decided to read it aloud, standing in front of our tree. As a gift, I asked Santa Claus to make you happier. I expected you to be content but instead you got so angry, because instead of asking for a gift for myself I only wanted your happiness.

It took years for me to understand that your discontent was a form of love for me and that you would have been happy just seeing *me* happy.

I would like to ask you if in your village you would have been more content than here in Rome, because there all the men have the same scars as you and you wouldn't have to hide them.

Do you miss it, Dad?

I would really like to know more about that village and all of Liberia. When will the war end? When will you be able to hug your brothers again? It's been such a long time since you've heard from them; it must be hard not knowing anything, having part of your own family in a country at war.

But if you knew, Dad, that you couldn't have found the answer in that glass that you turned around in your hands as though it were an oracle?

If you asked me, I would tell you that your relatives are safe and sound and that you will soon return to embrace them. Mom told me that your village is the most mystical in Liberia and magic is practiced there. I don't know if I believe in magic, but if you told me something about it maybe things would be different.

Mom also told me that my uncles are snake hunters and that you, when you were young, used to spend entire days in the forest. You don't know how much I would like to ask you what you used to do there, which animals you came across, if you had to face any dangers and how you got out of them.

What does it smell like in the forests where you used to hunt?

And what color is the sunset in your country?

I have only known one sunset: that of Rome.

I think of you as my father, but you're also a son and you were the first of ten siblings. You must have shouldered so many responsibilities from an early age.

You were the only one who left the village; you were courageous and went to Monrovia. Who knows if you were scared when you moved away from your family in search of a better future? Furthermore, you were also the only one in your family to come to Europe. Not only that, but you were also the first Liberian to come to Italy.

Who knows how you felt, if you were aware of your greatness and your courage, if joy or sadness prevailed in you, if you were afraid or you were a bold young African, ready to learn new things in life, even if not all of them were beautiful?

I know that so many people count on you now, not only us in the family, but also many friends and relatives. You take on everyone's burdens, forgetting that certain things are too much for one man, no matter how strong he is.

You could try saying no sometimes to others as well, not just to me.

Luckily there's music. It's a language that we both speak and we're able to understand each other more through musical notes than with words. Thanks to music, every now and then I see you smile and I can also communicate with you.

If I could write a letter to my father I'd tell him that I will understand many things only when I've finally managed to go to his village. Above all, I will understand how much he loved me.

And then I'd say that he was good when he decided to give up his dear and cold medicine friend, companion of so many thoughts. Many of his friends like him, far from home, did not make it. They let themselves be devoured by poison until they went insane.

5

If You Know Your History

Bob Marley's "Buffalo Soldier" talks about being stolen and taken to Africa. Dad listens to this song on repeat. *Se conoscessi la tua storia, allora sapresti da dove vieni.*

And he is always singing it, belting out the stolen-from-Africa part. Then I catch wind of him talking to himself, mulling over our story, his story—if only it weren't such a mystery to others.

I'm itching for him to tell me something.

He makes us listen to these songs and watch films that recount the stories of various African countries—but then he doesn't utter a word about himself.

I know the least about when they arrived in Italy and the initial years of my childhood. There are no photographs of that period at home, and I ask myself why. It's as if a piece of my life were missing; I don't know anything about myself until at least six years of age. Who knows what I was like as a newborn. Mom only ever showed me one photo of us twins at the age of one. We were inside one of those pens with a net around it, and we were dressed solely in white diapers that stood out against our Black skin. We are identical, so

Mom wrote our names on the photo in order to tell us apart. Anna on the left, Maria on the right.

I asked Mom where we were at that moment and she said, "At the embassy." Then little by little, she told me bits and pieces of the story.

My parents arrived in Italy at the end of the '70s with a man who would eventually become the Liberian ambassador.

Dad wasn't the first Kpelle man to come to Europe, but he was the only Kpelle man whose leaders allowed him to leave Wongbai, which nobody else had ever done before. There, everybody is family. Dad and Mom thought that they would be away for one year at most, just enough time to set aside some money to buy a house and some land upon their return to Liberia.

But things didn't go as planned.

I don't know what happened, but in our family album there are no photos of that time or of the ambassador and his family. Mom always tells us stories about her past and all the people she met. She has a good word to say about everyone, but she doesn't say much about the ambassador. And when she does, she is hardly nostalgic.

"With them, we hadn't a single day of rest. They would beckon us to do chores at any hour or minute of the day," she recounted, repeating many times that they were "Congo people," or rather Americo-Liberians who founded Liberia in 1821. They started to call the native Liberians Congo people after Great Britain abolished the slave trade, seizing ships of slaves leaving West Africa and returning them to Liberia and Sierra Leone, even if they didn't come from there. The fact that it was Africa was enough.

These newly released slaves that came from America were left in Liberia as the ships carrying them passed by the mouth of the Congo River—and for this reason they are called

Congo people. But they, the Americo-Liberians, felt more American than African. They dressed like Westerners, built houses similar to plantations in the American South, and preferred the English language, Christian religion, and monogamy. There was always conflict with the native Liberians.

Mom told me that one morning, she and Dad woke up and nobody was there. The ambassador and his whole family had left without warning and without my parents knowing. They escaped to America.

My parents had to postpone their plans of returning to Liberia and they continued to live at the embassy without receiving wages. They had to find new jobs and reinvent their life.

The loneliness of the early days was difficult for them, but among my mother's memories, her friendship with an Italian woman stands out. She was their first connection to this land.

She was called Anna Maria, and it's to her that my sister and I owe our names.

6
The Secret Diary

I don't even tell my deepest secrets to Maria.

Maybe I could share them with Dad if he weren't always so busy with work or music or his own musings. He and I are similar in this sense, and yet we never chat. In general, we don't talk a lot. I'm reserved, lost in the questions I want to ask my parents. But they are so many that I no longer know how to contain them.

Maria, on the other hand, is restless. She doesn't seem to have the same questions I do. Or maybe she does but prefers to keep moving forward.

Mom would like to return to Africa, even if only for vacation. I hear her talk about it with Dad, and she is forever telling us how wonderful it was to be there. Dad also agrees and I feel guilty for having been born in a country that isn't theirs and where we're only seen as foreigners. My parents should've only stayed in Italy a few years and then returned to Liberia to their families, but war broke out and they got stuck here, where every time we move we have to bring our documents that prove we have permission to be in Italy. Dad always tells us to keep our documents on us because more often than not they will ask for them. It makes me feel out of place. When somebody asks us questions or checks our documents, I'm silent and don't respond. I don't like to be observed because I know they watch me and every time eyes fall on me, it's as if time stands still.

Everybody thinks I'm shy and that I hide behind this timidity of mine, even if I don't really feel self-conscious. I just don't want to talk. By now my parents understand this, and it's probably the reason why they gave me a secret diary for Christmas.

Maria and I don't know if we ever believed in Santa Claus. We certainly don't believe in him now, even if some of our schoolmates are still convinced he exists. If we followed Liberian traditions, our Christmas would be very different from theirs. But our parents want us to be happy, so they try their best to do the same things they do in the homes of our friends. Dad buys a Christmas tree, although it's never big enough. It's not much taller than the living room chairs, and when we decorate it with Mom we don't even have to stand on our tippy toes. It's enough to stretch an arm. Our parents don't give us many presents, at most a gift each and a CD for both of us from Dad. My parents have many expenses. They have to send money to relatives who escaped the war and now live in Ghana. Even if I know Santa Claus doesn't exist, the fact that many other kids believe in him makes me doubt my beliefs, and so I ask Mom if it's true he's a made-up character.

She laughs and tells me about Africa.

There is also a sort of Santa Claus in Liberia, Old Man Beggar. He is elderly, a bit plump, and he goes from home to home before Christmas. But these are the only things they have in common. Old Man Beggar doesn't bring gifts to children, but rather he expects to receive an offering for the song and dance he performs to entertain you. Usually he is given something to eat and drink.

In Africa, Christmas is also a time when people get together with friends and family. They go to church and have parties. But Africa is big, and every country has its own traditions. Mom tells us about hers. Although she smiles, she always has slightly sad eyes when she reflects back on her childhood. She tells us that when she was a little girl they used to decorate little palm trees as if they were Christmas trees. And to exchange Christmas greetings, even today, everyone who meets stops and says, “Christmas is on you!” People who know each other race to see who can say it first. Christmas morning, the whole village comes together to sing. And when Mom was little, she woke up full of joy because she knew that they were going to sing after she received her present at home. In her village, they usually prefer to give useful gifts, such as soap, pencils, or notebooks for school and clothes to wear to church.

My parents think the secret diary is a useful gift for me, like those they give to Liberian children. Dad even said to me, “Write everything here.” Who knows if he also has his own diary, or if he just keeps his thoughts inside his head.

My diary has a light blue cover and there is a really cute snowman on it. But the most important thing is that it has a lock and a little key.

I started to use it right away. It was enough to open a little window inside of me and let a few words flow out. I don’t know if those white pages can respond to all of my questions, but when I write I feel better. I’m able to let go of all the thoughts that float through my mind each day. I write about school, my classmates, about how I feel when they call me *negra* and all those things I can’t say to anybody, not even to Maria, because even if she is identical to me, she doesn’t understand everything I tell her; or, maybe she doesn’t want to understand. She prefers to go for a run, to jump and do somersaults, while all I need is a white page to fill.

When I finish writing, I put on the lock and hide the diary in my closet, where I know that not even Mom will find it. I hide the key in my pillowcase so that I can be sure nobody will take it while I'm sleeping and stick their nose where it's not their business.

7
All the Relatives

When we were little, Maria and I were alone for a few hours in the afternoon after school or in the summer mornings because Mom and Dad had to work and there was no one to stay with us. We didn't like it, but little by little we got used to it: staying at home isn't hard. Just don't go out and don't open the door to strangers.

But now we have a house full of people and often we don't even know who they are. We can't decide if, when someone rings the doorbell, we should open the door or not; sometimes we can't even sleep in our bed because someone else is in it. My parents always tell me that every African I see or meet, even in the street, is part of the family. For us, every African is an uncle or an aunt, an older brother or a sister, a cousin. This is the reason why there are always so many people in our house. And they're not just from Liberia but from all over Africa: Sierra Leone, Mozambique, Ethiopia, and other countries, some of which I hadn't heard of before meeting them.

I really like the idea that my family is big. I like to finally feel part of something. I like to feel African like my uncles, aunties, and parents do, but I don't know all these people and I don't know why they all come to our house, which isn't even that big.

When Mom and Dad go to work, they tell us that at home the aunties and uncles are in charge and that we must show respect. I call the women who are more or less Mom's age aunties. To tell you the truth, I don't exactly know how old Mom is. Every year we celebrate her birthday by guessing a random age. She tells us that she is the same age as the aunties or that she is slightly older than them. Calendars don't exist in her village. And of course, you know that Black people never age. On the other hand, we call the younger girls sis, the older ones sister, and that's fine with them. Some of these people have children and we consider them cousins. I share my things with them: toys, clothes, and even my bed because Mom said that it's the right thing to do.

Still, something doesn't add up to me.

Certain clothes and toys are mine and I don't even want Maria to touch them, and this is typically okay with Mom. And usually, we all sleep in our own beds but not now. Why is changing all this suddenly acceptable?

Why can't I too sleep on the sofa bed in the living room and get up later than usual?

I don't ask Mom anything and I don't even talk about it with Maria. She seems content; she's happy and she laughs even when we sleep in the living room and in the middle of the night some auntie slips under the covers and takes up all the space with that big butt of hers.

Too bad that none of the people we host speak Italian well. I know a little bit of pidgin English that my parents taught me, and with that we're able to understand each other.

I also learn many new words from various African languages, which sound nice to me.

Another advantage of having all these people at home is the food. There's always something ready to eat, someone who's cooking African dishes, spicy and flavorful. The aunties are often at the stove: they cook legumes, vegetables, meat, and fish. I found out that my favorite dish is *jollof* rice, which is a rice-based dish with chicken and lots of vegetables. I really like it; it's a little sweet and it's orange in color, probably because you make it with lots of carrots and there's some tomato too. When they cook it, I always have a big helping and the aunties seem satisfied with that. But I'm not the only one who likes it. Some people even eat it for breakfast. Jollof rice is so spicy and fragrant that its smell lingers in the kitchen for days and it always makes me feel like it's a holiday, a special time.

Every auntie has her own particular dish, different from all the others, that she learned to make in a faraway land that shapes its taste and smell and now all of these fragrances are in my house mixed with the noise and gestures that make me feel a part of it.

Of all the aunties who hang around the house my favorite is Auntie Harriet.

She is Liberian, she's always smiling, she has a pretty face, and she must weigh about a hundred kilos. The funny thing is that at least eighty of those hundred kilos are found on her big, upturned butt, which bounces all over the place when she moves. She likes to be with us kids and she often tickles us on the neck and we laugh so much with her. She also cooks yummy meals, especially rice with sauce and meat, fried bananas, and cassava. But we mustn't say that what she makes is tastier because the other aunties might get offended. But Auntie Harriet knows this and often when she's cooking, she winks at us and we know that she's cooking for us.

The strictest is Auntie Janet. She yells at us a lot and wants us to keep our rooms very clean and tidy. Sometimes I complain to Mom because I don't like to be yelled at, but Mom tells me that we must obey her. She told us that Auntie Janet is so serious because she had to grow up quickly. When she was our age, she became pregnant by her uncle. These details are difficult to understand and I don't really know what it means, but since Mom told me this I try to be good with her.

What is certain is that delicious food is never lacking in our house now. And there is no shortage of company.

Some people stay only a few days, then they leave and we never see them again. On the other hand, others stay a long time and it seems to me that they're really part of the family now, because I get used to having them at home. There are also those who just come to meet Mom and Dad, who I guess have become famous or important—or both—for this big family.

Auntie Harriet will be leaving soon too, she told me. And other uncles and aunties who have been here a long time will also be leaving.

It made me a little sad and Auntie Harriet sensed this. She told me that they're going to go to America because we're all children of America and sooner or later all Liberians want to go there. I never thought of going there myself one day; my parents don't talk about it. Dad thinks that it's even America's fault that Liberia is going through a crisis, and that's why Liberians around the world want to go there, as if

America has to solve their problems, as if America owes them something.

My parents talk about Italy and Africa but not America.

Who knows what the aunties and uncles will find there, where they will live, and if there will be another family there like ours that will welcome them and another kitchen to fill with African smells, foods, and colors?

Who knows if they know that America is even farther away than Italy and that the journey to go back, back to Africa, is much longer? But perhaps they don't think about Liberia anymore, like my parents; they don't think about going back.

And me? When I'm grown up, where will I go?

8
The Kpelle People

I met my dad's best friends when I was very little; I'd say that they have practically always been in my life. They are like brothers to each other, and to my sister and me they are like uncles. They've all lived in Italy for a while now, like my parents.

Uncle Isacco and Uncle Robert are Liberian like Dad, but they all come from different districts and villages. Uncle Samba, on the other hand, is from Sierra Leone.

Uncle Robert's last name is Freeman, "free man," and that's what everyone calls him. Our father always told us to pay attention to surnames and also to first names because each one has a meaning that guides you through life. He told us that Uncle Robert's was given to people during the time when there was still slavery.

Our surname, on the other hand, has not changed over time. It has remained the same: Gehnyei. My grandparents and our great-grandparents fought hard so that it wouldn't be changed. Uncle Isacco and Dad speak the same dialect and they have the same traditions because their villages are very close, even if my father's is considered the village of sorcerers and it can't be easy at all to live there. One time I saw that Uncle Isacco also has scars on his back that are similar to Dad's, even if his are more numerous and a little wider. I glanced at him as he quickly put on a shirt, but since I know my father doesn't want to talk about it, I've never even asked my uncle anything, thinking that for him too it's something he prefers not to talk about.

We don't see Uncle Isacco often. He only visits us during vacations because he doesn't live in Rome but in Porto Empedocle, in the province of Agrigento. Everyone knows him as the Liberian who saves the lives of refugees landing in Sicily. He helps all people but especially those who come from Ghana, the same country that his wife, Equa, is from. He always says that living in Agrigento for him is like living in Liberia, even if I've never asked him why.

When Uncle Isacco is at our place there are always so many happy times, not only because me and Maria have a lot of fun with him, but also because we see that Dad is happy hanging out with his good friend.

When they talk they remember their childhood and their villages and they think back above all about the nice things that they left. It's almost like they're back in Liberia when they reminisce. Me and my sister, on the other hand, can't wait for our uncle to perform traditional dances with us. It's a game that Mom told us we started playing when we were barely crawling: he gets in front of us and we follow him like ducklings behind mamma duck. We follow his steps and repeat his words, even if we are ignorant of their meaning. One of the many funny things about Uncle Isacco is that he speaks to us in Kpelle (his and Dad's language spoken by the Kpelle people in Africa) as well as in Sicilian. He and Dad always make fun of each other because they both learned the dialect of the city where they live instead of standard Italian. It's nice, however, that they both do everything to keep the sounds of their homeland alive, even if it's always been strange to hear them talking and laughing, and I have no idea what they're saying to each other.

But Papa and Uncle Isacco's isn't the only African language I've heard spoken. Uncle Samba and his wife Alice speak Krio and it's the language that I like the most and that, by dint of being with them and asking questions, I started to speak a little too. I find it very fun. Uncle Samba is the oldest uncle, and the thing that has always seemed strange to us is that even after being in Italy for such a long time, even before my father, he's never learned one word of Italian. He's always said that he doesn't want to learn the Italian language because sooner or later he'll go back to Africa. The others have always told him that it's important to know a little Italian, but he doesn't want to hear about it. And this concerns not only the Italian language but also Italian habits. In fact, he doesn't even eat pasta and bread but only the Sierra Leonean dishes that Aunt Alice cooks for him. Uncle Samba is a very tall man and he always wears dark suits because he's the driver for African ambassadors who live in Rome. Uncle Samba used to be the driver for the Liberian ambassador too, and that's how Dad and Uncle Samba met. He really likes to dance and I've always liked to watch him, how he moves, so tall, though when he's done dancing he always has to wipe off a great deal of sweat with the towel Auntie Alice carries around for him.

Uncle Robert, on the other hand, is the troublemaking uncle. He's never liked being told what to do, not even when the cops stop him in the street for a document check and he always reacts badly when someone calls him "negro." My dad tells him not to get offended because it's well known that in Italy, they can't stand a Black man driving around in a cool car like the one he has. But Uncle Robert can't ignore it and his looks don't help him to go unnoticed. He's big and strong and everyone says he looks like the boxer Mike Tyson. Me and Maria have a lot of fun wrestling with him: we climb onto his shoulders for a piggyback ride. I pull him on one side and my sister on the other; he's so strong that we're sure he won't get hurt. I've never understood what he does for work. Sometimes he disappears for days and everyone worries about him because they're afraid that something bad has happened to him. Only Dad, while listening to Bob Marley, tells everyone not to worry because Freeman is a free man and does as he pleases.

9
The Initiation

While all the aunties are visiting, I have my first period. One morning I stumble to the bathroom barely awake, as I usually do. But this time I find my underwear soaked with blood. My arms and legs go weak and I'm scared I might be sick. I don't want to cry. I don't want them to suspect anything, so I immediately lock the bathroom door for fear of being found out. I don't really know what it is. I've heard people talk about menstruation. That must be it! But how does it work and what am I supposed to do?

Without exactly understanding why, it seems important to hide what happened to me.

At times I have overheard the aunties talking in the kitchen about the moment when a girl becomes a woman. They say it's by the age of eleven in Africa. I'm almost twelve years old, so what does that make me?

I slowly calm myself down. I race to my bedroom to get a clean pair of underwear, and then I return to the bathroom. I put them on and roll up a wad of toilet paper, stuffing it into my panties. Then I take the dirty underwear, wash them carefully with hand soap, and put them out to dry in the sun.

That morning, however, Auntie Janet got up early to prepare *torta di mais*, the corn cake she promised me she would make the night before. She begins to call my mom and other aunties from the kitchen.

I hear her chant something, repeating it over and over again. I get closer and I understand her words as clear as day: "Eh, eh, my people, someone here just got her period and she is hiding it oh oh oh." She repeats these words in an endless loop.

Mom told us that although Italians usually don't tell others when they get their period, in Liberia an event as important as one's first menstruation is celebrated with all of the women in the village. It's usually a mother, an auntie, or a sister who announces the occasion, singing as they move from one house to the next. According to their customs, this will help the girl mature.

Yet that song of theirs annoys me. I run to my bed and cover my ears with a pillow, hoping to keep those words at bay. But I can't escape Auntie Harriet's shrill voice. She calls the others to the bathroom. Maria is also in our bedroom, strangely silent and still. Mom opens our door and summons us into her room, a place we usually don't go unless she calls us there.

Maria and I move slowly. I don't want to go and I don't think she does either.

As soon as we enter, we see all the aunties sitting in a circle waiting for us. I feel sick to my stomach and I want to cry. But I fight back my tears, because I don't want it to seem like I did something wrong, even if I know I hid a big secret from Mom and the aunties.

Auntie Harriet holds the dirty underpants in her hand. I don't want to see them. Why doesn't she put them away?

And I thought I washed them well. How the heck is there still a stain on them?

Mom looks at us with tenderness and asks, "Do you have something to tell me?"

I reply no in a soft voice, almost a whisper. Maria sits in silence. Mom then asks us a second time. Maria and I don't say anything. I can't lower my eyes or they'll realize that it's me who is hiding something.

Mom doesn't believe us, and our aunties also sense we are lying through our teeth.

Auntie Harriet gives us one of her contagious smiles and in her lovely loud voice she asks us, "Do you know what is happening to your body?"

And Mom adds, "You can tell the truth. There are no secrets between any of us. This is an event that will change your life."

Auntie Janet chimes in and parrots Mom and Auntie Harriet: "You know, it's nothing bad. It'll surely change your lives. Tell us the truth."

What really dumbfounds me is that Maria doesn't say a word, she who usually speaks freely and is always ready to protest when she doesn't like something.

But why isn't she saying anything and acting like me?

Mom, however, instills a sense of peace with her sweet voice.

"Do you remember the story I told you about the girls whose bodies suddenly develop and they grow up? Well, now one of you is no longer a little girl, and it's for this reason that we have come together with your aunts. We are all women here because today is an important occasion. You are big girls now, ready for new changes, and not only physical ones. So don't be scared and tell me, which one of you has your period?"

"Me," we respond in unison.

We look at one another astonished. Once again we are living the same experience.

We are two souls, so different yet destined to share everything that happens to us.

In the past, we always had a fever together, as well as bronchitis and chicken pox. And now we are menstruating together. Even our transition from girlhood to womanhood happened at the same time. Neither of us was left behind, neither of us ventured into unknown territory without the other. And both of us tried to hide our periods in the same way.

"I noticed something strange in both of you," Mom professes.

Auntie Janet tells us that when she had her first period she was petrified, but at the same time she was happy to have become a woman. She knew she could share the news with the rest of the village without having to utter more than a few words.

And then she adds, "The eyes of a *femmina* talk when something is changing inside of her."

She also tells us about the time she got pregnant, but at a certain point she stops and breathes deeply and continues: "From now on you can have children and for this reason you must be careful with men."

Mom opens one of her drawers, takes out some pads, and shows us how to use them.

Getting my first period didn't make me feel more grown up, but sharing this moment with Mom and the aunties was precious, and it made me feel a bit more womanly, like them. We finally settle down and Auntie Janet senses it. She gives us a big smile and says, "Well, I think we need to celebrate here. How do you feel about a nice slice of torta di mais?"

10
La Lingua Parlata

Ever since all the aunties and uncles left for America, the house feels empty.

There used to be chaos at every hour of the day and maybe also at night, when I was sleeping. I don't know how late the adults would stay up, but it was fun having so many people around the house. Maria and I didn't have to stay home alone all afternoon. Even though we're used to being by ourselves, there has been some new energy around lately. Pola, one of Mom's friends, came to live at our house. Mom told us she would be our babysitter, and I like the idea of having a person who comes to pick us up at school and spends time with us.

Pola is Jamaican, like the music Dad puts on and that me and Maria like to dance to. When Dad plays music, the living room becomes our stage. We prance around the table, usually laughing, and although we wreak a bit of havoc, even Dad smiles.

Mom told us that Pola no longer has documents because a woman stole them from her, so she will stay with us until

La Lingua Parlata (Spoken Language).

they find them. I don't even know where she calls home. Maybe she doesn't like to live by herself so Mom, who is a good friend, invited her to come sleep with me and my sister in our bedroom.

Pola has short hair and lighter skin than us, although she isn't white like my schoolmates. She's so skinny, with stick legs and a flat stomach. Pola is completely different from the aunties who lived with us before, with their big butts that take up a lot of space. They knew how to cook really well, and they always had something on the stove. Pola, on the other hand, is a disaster in the kitchen and she only knows how to make sweet potatoes and cod fritters. But aside from this, I really like being with her. She is young and dresses a lot like a teenager: miniskirts, belly-baring tops, boots, a ton of bracelets, and gold earrings. She speaks English, but in a different way than Mom and Dad, and also Simona, our English teacher. Pola always seems angry when she talks. In the beginning, it seemed like she really didn't want to spend time with us. I didn't think I liked her, but then I realized that it's just her way of being in the world and she isn't really annoyed—quite the opposite.

When she comes to pick us up at school, everyone hears her say, "Wah gwaan, twins?" But nobody besides us understands what she's saying because they don't understand the phrase, "How are you, twins?" and even if it's an easy question, it's heartwarming to hear her say it in a language that none of my classmates know.

When Pola came to our house, I didn't think that, among the many things she brought with her, she'd have so many CDs.

She often makes us listen to her music, and straightaway I noticed that it's different than Dad's music. He has many vinyl records and likes reggae, afrobeat, and all African music, really. Pola also likes Dad's music, as well as hip-hop and R&B. She said she wants to teach Maria and me how to rap, and I can't wait. But first we have to learn a few songs, even those really really dated ones that she calls "old school."

She has the CDs of Public Enemy, Missy Elliott, Lauryn Hill, and many other singers. Her favorite song is "Mary Had a Little Boy" by a group called Snap. Maria and I learned all the words. First we listened to it many many times, and then Pola wrote the words on a piece of paper and she made us repeat them until we no longer needed the paper and knew the song by heart. It was a bit like at school when they made us learn poetry and then we had to recite it in front of the class, only that with Pola it's more fun because we get to sing. I sing the first part of the song and Maria the second part, and we all sing the refrain together. We feel like a real duo, and we focus ambitiously on our act. Pola also made us watch the video of Snap performing, with all the dancers moving very quickly. I also learned some of the steps, but I'm a slower dancer than they are. And I'm pretty shy and only dance when nobody is watching.

But I don't get shy when we dance in the little shows that we rehearse with Pola. She turns on the big stereo—the one that plays tapes, CDs, and records—that Maria and I aren't allowed to touch in case we break it. Pola, however, has permission to use it. She puts on music and all three of us dance. She taught us a little dance, like in school recitals, even if the moves are very different than the ones our teacher taught us. Pola said that the steps we learn at school are for "white kids," while the dance routine that she teaches us is hip-hop, a completely different thing because we really have to move our bodies.

In order to prepare for our little show, we started rummaging through the closet, and we even went through the clothes that don't fit us anymore. Pola pulled out all the colorful shirts and skirts she could find. Some of them Mom never lets us put on. I don't even know who gave them to us; I don't think she bought them for us. Some of the clothes are too small for us, but we put them on anyway, even if it isn't easy to fit into them. All three of us like to admire ourselves in the mirror. We are dressed in miniskirts, even if the ones Maria and I have on are longer than Pola's. Hers is so short that you can see her underwear when she dances.

We make our way to the living room to start the rehearsal. Maria and I move the couches. They are rather light, and it was enough to push them slightly into the corners. Pola moves the table and chairs so that we have more space to dance. The most important thing is to put everything back before Mom gets home. She doesn't want us to go too wild because she's afraid that we'll hurt ourselves. Maria and I love to put on these little dances for Mom and Dad. They are our audience and when we perform, they always shower us with praise.

But with Pola we don't only think about dancing. Sometimes we venture out on a bike ride or we grab a *gelato* for our afternoon snack.

The only thing we can't do with our babysitter is our homework because Pola only speaks English and she can't help us with Italian grammar issues. And she can't help us with math or science either, because she doesn't understand the topics we have to study. The teachers always tell us that our homework isn't done well because we speak too much English at home. Sometimes we also speak English at school by mistake, and not only among ourselves. The teachers tell us we must only speak Italian at school.

11
Mussolini the Italian

Every morning, Maria and I leave the house together. Sometimes we take the bus and other times, like this morning, we walk. We stroll side by side until we get to the hill. Maria doesn't slow down but I feel all the weight of my backpack filled with books and I move slowly, one step in front of the other, lost in thought.

When we finally near the school I see some of my classmates coming out of the pizzeria; they've bought a snack for later. They eat their pizza during recess, but I don't get a weekly allowance, even though I would like to. Every once in a while, my parents happen to leave some change on the kitchen table and then I can be like my friends during recess and have pizza too, but most mornings it's not like that and I just have to wait to go home and eat. Now, in middle school, we leave at the end of the morning and have lunch at home. Today, unfortunately, I don't have any money.

But this is not the only difference from before. Elementary school had some nice classrooms, but in this one they're small and everything is older and sad, gray. There's also a courtyard here where we sometimes have recess; I can see it from my classroom window. It's different from the nice courtyard with trees that I was able to see from the window of our elementary school. Now I see a lonely, dried up mimosa tree and a few tufts of grass. The desks are old and some are broken; they wobble when we sit on them and write. They are arranged in rows in front of the teacher's desk. There's a blackboard behind the desk and above it hangs a crucifix from which Jesus seems to gaze and who knows what he thinks of certain professors. Every once in a while I look at that crucifix and even if I'm not baptized and we don't go to church on Sundays, I know who Jesus is because our parents make us study religion, like everyone in class.

The morning bell rings. I sit next to Maria in my spot in the second row. We've been together in the same class since the first year of middle school. Now we're in the third year and, like every year, we're the only Black students in the school.

Her and me, me and her.

The math teacher arrives and today she's wearing a long, colorful dress with little flowers with a black jacket over it. She has short dark hair, and to me at thirteen she looks almost old, much older than my parents. I think she's over fifty.

I still remember the first time I saw her. On the first day of middle school she presented herself in the classroom with the roster under her arm, and standing next to the desk she inspected all of us, one by one, lingering a little more on Maria and I.

"I'm your math teacher, Edda Milani. My father named me Edda, like Mussolini's daughter. And if there's something that I can't stand it's immigrants who think they're Italian."

I heard my classmates quietly repeat the name Mussolini, with those hissing esses. I didn't say anything, while Maria asked me in a low voice, "Our parents are immigrants, right?" I nodded my head.

The teacher saw us and immediately told us to be quiet.

Things haven't changed much since that day.

However much effort Maria and I make, to her we are only the daughters of immigrants who think they're Italian. Even if we were born in Italy, she can't see anything else and there are many days when she enters the classroom and the first thing she says is that Italy belongs to the Italians.

In class Ms. Milani moves like a soldier and her manner of speaking frightens me. We always ask each other what she'll have to say as soon as she enters the classroom. Everyone at school knows she has a problem with us; even the principal knows it. Over the last two years we got bad grades in math, but we passed, perhaps because we did very well in other subjects. The third year is harder though. There's so much to study and Ms. Milani is even stricter this year.

Me and Maria try to arrive prepared with our math homework. We make an effort to study everything, even though the expressions and equations are difficult, but we always get Ds in that class.

For today we had to do some exercises that neither one of us grasped.

Maria raises her hand and asks the teacher if she can explain again how to solve the equations she has assigned. She replies that we don't understand because we are the daughters of immigrants.

"Everyone knows that immigrants are people who don't know how to do anything. And therefore it's logical that the children of immigrants don't know how to do anything."

And after having responded to us like that, she begins to explain a new topic, one of the last ones before the test, and I already know that I will not understand anything.

Luckily, this afternoon me and Maria are invited over to Simona's house and Alessandra will also be there. They're nerds and from a middle-class right-wing family, and there are some classmates who mock them in an unkind way and I feel a little sorry for them because even if they always wear Ralph Lauren clothes they are kind to us and they often invite us to study in their villas in the fancy Olgiata neighborhood.

When we're at their house, me and Maria usually feel a little uncomfortable because they have bedrooms as big as our living room at home, and I would like a room all for myself too; I would even be content with a smaller one. When we go there to study, we see that they have domestic help who take care of the cleaning and gardening, and there's even a Filipino nanny.

I already know that this afternoon Simona's mom will give us a snack. She does it every time and they are always delicious: cinnamon rolls with Nutella, chocolate muffins, pizza rolls, or ham sandwiches. She'll also give us fruit juice, which I like very much and we almost never have at our house. My stomach is already grumbling just thinking about all of these yummy treats. To get to Simona's house, me and Maria take the bus, but afterward they bring us home in their great big car.

I don't know why our classmates and their moms do all of this for us. Maybe it makes them feel good; maybe they think that it's the right thing to do. Whatever the motive, it makes for some really nice afternoons. Our two classmates have already helped us so much in math and today we hope that they will teach us what the teacher assumed we wouldn't understand.

When she's done explaining, Ms. Milani gives us back the last homework assignment we completed. When she gets to us, she puts it on the desk without saying a word. No comment about immigrants, nothing. And she doesn't even look at us. Me and Maria take our assignments and we realize that there are fewer red marks and corrections than usual, and we turn the paper over: C+.

12
The Diamond Princess

Once upon a time, there was an elegant woman with deep eyes and very black hair. She came from a faraway land that she had left as a little girl to follow her dreams and her love. That land, however, was always in her heart, but she couldn't go back there because it was ruled by an evil queen named war who had taken away all the joy from the people who lived there—and even from the woman who had gone far away.

She had tried to invent a new happiness, but it wasn't easy because she lived in the kingdom of backwards colors. Her skin was dark as night and soft as silk, while the skin of the others was as pale as the winter dawn.

When she was little and lived in her country and war was just a thought that nobody had yet brought to fruition, she had many animals to play with, even fawns with slender, snappy legs. Her father was a hunter but he didn't kill all the animals that he flushed out; some he preferred to bring home with him and give to his children. She and her siblings loved to play with the puppies that their father brought them, but they also played with all the nature at their feet. Close to the house there was a river with shiny little pebbles. She and her brother collected them and put them into long rows on which the sun shone, rendering them bright as stars. When they had finished playing, they would throw those stones back into the river, which looked after them.

One day some strange men arrived. Their skin didn't have any color, and there was no one in the village as light-skinned as they were. They talked a lot with the father about the little girl; they didn't want to buy the animals that they were hunting. They brought gifts that they said were good things to eat, but they didn't come from trees or the land, let alone from the forest. They came in gray cans with images on them that no one had ever seen before. They said it was fish, but fish come from the river or the sea, not from gray cans. They had also brought an even stranger gift that they called tobacco. You weren't supposed to eat it, and nobody really knew what it was for, but they said that it was good. Those gifts, however, said the father to his little girl, could only be his if he gave them some of the stones from the river. They didn't want all of them, just the shiny ones that the children enjoyed and that tickled their toes when they entered the water.

The little girl didn't understand why those men without any color were so interested in their games and only when she got older did she discover that the shiny pebbles in the river had a name of their very own; they were called diamonds.

Mom, why don't you tell me stories of when you were little?

Why don't you play with me, Mom?

The other moms play with their daughters and even tell them fairy tales. But I could never believe those stories because their stories are white, just like how their skin is white. They are written especially for them, with pale pink fairies or gnomes and cold snowy winters.

Mom, where you come from everything is in color, not only skin. There aren't winters nor is there snow that blankets the land in white and dampens the colors. And then there's nature, and for every animal, every plant, the entire village respects the cycle.

Mom, tell me about Martuaken, about your village. Let me feed on your stories as I fed on the milk from your breast. I'm hungry for my roots. I need to know where I come from.

Mom, what was it like to find yourself living in the land of backwards colors?

I see you when you come home from work, tired, after having spent the day in the houses of women who have different skin than you; you clean their rooms and you iron their clothes. You are at their beck and call, but when you come home you are also at the service of your family and friends. You take care of all those in need, as if always being available were a mission.

Nevertheless, I read in your eyes the heavy weight you carry inside of you, a pain that I'm too small to relieve but that, if I could, I would carry on my own shoulders to be able to see you smile, at least once.

You don't complain and you don't tell me anything, but I know that if you were able to tell me what pains you, then you would feel better.

If you could, you would tell me that your heart can't find peace, but you prefer to suffer in silence because it's not right that I take on your pain; it would be like harming me and you don't want that.

Mom, if we talked about your life, I would tell you that I admire your determination and your tenacity in taking care of our family. You are our rock and you make yourself seem happy, so as not to disturb our childhood and our right to serenity.

I am your daughter; this is my role, but your history renders me grown. It doesn't really allow me to be a child. I would like to take your place to free you from that boulder that you carry in your heart. I would like to be able to say to you, "I got this."

I need to hear your voice.

Tell me a fairy tale; tell me the story of that elegant woman with deep eyes and the darkest hair.

13
The Power of Twins

Uncle Joe is my mom's youngest brother. He is handsome and always laughing. And he looks like Denzel Washington. Uncle recently arrived in Italy. He doesn't live with us, but he comes to visit us during the weekends. He wears tight pants and chic shirts. He goes to the disco with his friends—and he has *a lot* of friends.

Mom doesn't like Uncle's friends. She only likes Bintu, his best friend. Mom said that Bintu is a good person. She is from Sierra Leone and she is really kind, as well as tall and much blacker than us. And when she sees us she says: "Oh this pikins are growing," which in Krio means that Maria and I, little girls, are getting older.

I love my uncle very much. Every time he comes to visit, he gives us money to buy candy and chips with a surprise in the bag. Uncle Joe drives us around in Dad's car, even if Dad isn't a fan of this idea because Uncle Joe doesn't have his license. We cruise around the neighborhood and stop at a bar where Uncle orders a beer. In his car, he makes us listen to all the songs he dances to with his friends, songs like "Shut Up" by the Black Eyed Peas and "Angel" by Shaggy, the beats of Busta Rhymes, and a lot of other tunes he calls house music. When Uncle Joe comes to our house, he asks us if we have been good, and he tells us not to make Mom and Dad mad because they work very hard to support us. Even when he leaves, he tells us to behave ourselves or he won't take us out and let us listen to his music.

Now our uncle is engaged to Sia. She is Liberian like us. Mom said that Sia is from another village that's called Lofa County. I don't like Sia. She says many mean things to us. She tells us that in Africa twins are dangerous and that we scare people because our eyes are so big.

She tells us we are witches, dangerous little twins, because twins make magic and read people's future.

Mom said that we mustn't believe a word Sia says.

Since Uncle Joe got engaged to her, he doesn't give us money anymore, and he doesn't drive us around in his car.

Today we stayed at home with Uncle Joe and Sia. Uncle went out to buy cigarettes while Sia watched television in the living room. So Maria and I played a prank on her. Because she always says nasty things to us, Maria and I told her that we really are witches and that we want to read her future. Sia, unsurprisingly, only wanted to hear good news. We took her hand and pretended to read her palm. We convinced her that she wouldn't live very long.

I wanted to laugh because you could see that she fell for it, but I kept a straight face, like Maria, and pretended I was a witch. Maria stroked Sia's hand gently and told her that she wanted the couple to make some little cousins together, but that her hand showed they wouldn't have a single child. While Maria talked, I pretended to be sad as I read along with her. Sia asked us if there was something else written on her palm, and we told her we couldn't see anything.

Then Uncle Joe returned to our house and he and Sia went home a little while later.

Not long after, though, he called Mom and told her that we scared Sia because we convinced her she would die prematurely. Mom yelled at us because these are things you just don't say. Maria and I replied that it was only a joke and that we played it on her because Sia always tells us we are witches.

"You don't mess around with these things," Mom insisted. "There are some Africans who really believe everything twins say. Twins are powerful and it's for this reason they are so special."

In the end, Mom started laughing. She said that her twins pulled a fast one this time and now Sia doesn't want to come over ever again.

14
The First Sister

Today my sister Comfort arrives in Rome.

I have another sister besides Maria. She is older than me and I can't wait to meet her. They told us very little about her. Maybe it's too difficult for Mom to talk about it. She said that she stayed in Africa with Grandma Jessie, my mom's mother, and that they were among the few who survived the war.

A few weeks ago we received a call. The phone wouldn't stop ringing, but my parents weren't home and our aunts didn't want to pick up because, even if they live with us, it wasn't their house. But at a certain point, given the insistence, Aunt Harriet took the call and on the other end there was a person, from Africa, who was looking for Mom. She was still at work and Aunt Harriet told them to call back later. (Auntie still hasn't left for the United States; they haven't given her a visa yet. Nonetheless, she says she will leave soon.) Aunt Harriet told us she could tell something was wrong because the person on the line talked so frantically.

When the phone rang again, the day after, Dad was at home. He had returned home from work first. It was one of Mom's old aunts calling to tell us that Grandma Jessie had died and my sister Comfort was now all alone. My parents had left my sister Comfort with our grandmother, who raised her during the war. After Grandma passed away, Comfort disappeared. They found her wandering around a run-down market looking for something to eat.

Dad and Aunt Harriet didn't know what to tell Mom. Who could predict how she would react given that she is so far away from Comfort and her mom is no longer alive?

The day after, our old aunt from Africa called again. Nobody had said a word to Mom yet. But this time she picked up the phone before anyone else.

"Eliza, is that you? I've been calling to inform you about your mother."

"What's wrong with my mother?"

As Mom continued listening, a look of shock and dismay came over her. The phone fell from her hand and she collapsed to the ground, crying desperately.

I had never seen Mom cry before, and certainly not like that, on the floor beating her hands on the tiles while speaking her language.

I didn't know what to do. I wanted to hug her but I understood that her pain was too great to contain. I also started crying, in silence, without really understanding what was happening in Liberia.

When Dad managed to calm her down, they sat together to decide what to do next. Somebody had to fetch Comfort right away, or she risked disappearing altogether.

A few days later, Mom was able to get herself together and buy an airplane ticket to Liberia. She left to go collect that little girl they called Comfort, who was meant to be their comfort but for many years remained alone in Africa as a result of the war that divided us.

And now *eccola qua*, my big sister is here!

When I meet her for the first time, she's wearing a shirt and a pair of jeans. Comfort is very skinny, her clothes are baggy, and she seems uneasy. Right away, the combat boots she has on catch my eye. In Liberia, they call them soldier shoes. Mom made her wear them because they have a thick sole and laces you can tie nice and tight. Comfort had never worn a pair of shoes before and Mom was afraid that if she put on a normal pair of shoes, she would take them off and wind up barefoot.

The first words I hear her say, and that I'm able to understand, are her complaints that the boots are too tight. Mom tells her that before she can take the boots off, she has to say hello to her sisters, but she rebuts that before she can do anything, she's gotta take off her shoes.

While she unties her long laces, Maria and I huddle next to her smiling.

"Ya hello-o," she says to us, and we sit still and observe her.

I get the impression that she doesn't really want to get to know us or be friends. But maybe it's too early. Nevertheless, she must be happy to be with her family, since she was so far away for many years.

When Comfort is finally able to get her boots off, I notice that her feet have a different shape than those of Maria and me. Who knows how many miles she walked, barefoot, or how many borders she crossed and streets she braved alone. On her soles she has big calluses. I exchange looks with Maria; we pretend everything is normal so that we don't make her feel uncomfortable.

But Comfort doesn't get embarrassed easily. She doesn't seem to notice certain things, or rather she just doesn't care about them. And so, the state of her feet is our problem, not hers.

Maria and I show her the room and the bed we made for her, with the help of Aunt Harriet, in the days we awaited her arrival, days that never seemed to end without Mom or a word of news.

Mom starts cooking right away and she makes a plate of *spaghetti al ragù*. She tells Comfort that she has to start getting used to Italian dishes, now that she lives here.

But Comfort whines because the worm-like spaghetti make her feel queasy. She hasn't stopped complaining since she arrived a few hours ago, and for everyone at home it's as if she were an only child. Mom ends up preparing her some *pennette*, a short cylinder-shaped pasta, which she finds slightly more pleasing but not enough to entice her to eat everything on her plate.

At a certain point during that unusual dinner, Dad turns on the television and flicks from one channel to the next until he settles on the news.

Among the slew of news stories, they discuss Africa as images of famished children flicker across the screen. They instantly capture Comfort's attention. She gets up and moves toward the TV. She doesn't know the language the journalist is speaking, but she understands what it's about; images speak louder than words and it's a language she seems to understand well. She asks Dad to change the channel because it's fruitless to watch and talk about it: nobody will save those children.

She doesn't seem sad or scared. It's as if her gaze has been stoked like a flame.

Without having to ask, she tells us about a time she lined up outside a missionary church alongside hundreds of other children. They waited a long time for them to open the gates and give them something to eat. But there were too many people, so when they finally opened up, they could only feed a few hungry mouths.

Then she doesn't say another word, and I start to think of all the things I don't know about her life, things I never really thought about before.

15
Rocks in Our Shoes

Today is a hot day and me and my sisters would like to jump in the pool.

It's Sunday and there's nobody in the office. Even the pool is empty, but we can't go in. We can't even go into the big courtyard. I often look at it from the gate and I think that if I had a dog it could run free in that great big space and I would throw them a ball and this is how we would pass the time.

We moved a couple months ago. Dad is no longer a bricklayer; he works as the caretaker of a pharmaceutical company and we live in a house close to the entry gate and when someone buzzes he checks their info and if all is well he opens the gate. Dad mows the lawn, takes in the mail, cleans the pool, paints the walls, and every day he lets in the people who come to the office. The company is in a large green area with many fruit trees, palm trees, roses, and other plants. But my gaze always ends up at the swimming pool. It's not easy when it's hot like today, seeing the reflection of the sun in that blue water at an arm's reach, imagining how refreshing it would be and I'm not even allowed to dip a toe in.

But we're the caretaker's daughters. No pool. No running on the lawn. No dog.

Moving to this house was a nice change, because before we had to go everywhere on foot or by bus, but now even to go get a gelato Dad has to come with us. But me and Maria are sixteen and our sister Comfort is even older than we are and we would like to be independent, to get around on our own. So we decide to bike to Grottarossa Park. We have three bicycles, one for each of us. Two are pretty new but the third is somewhat broken, paint is missing in certain places, and when you brake it makes an annoying sound.

And I'm always the one who has to ride it. We take the shortcut, riding quickly through the fields; we take it to get to Papacci Park and then get out of the sun and cool off under the trees.

We hang out there almost every afternoon. We sit on one of the many benches, we watch the boys playing on the soccer field, and we drink fresh water from the fountain.

Other times we walk around Grottarossa Park, lock our bicycles to a pole, and set off on foot. We stay close to each other and we laugh but it often happens that the impulse to laugh fades because when we pass by the arcade there are some boys who treat us badly, very badly. We immediately sense when some kids have mean intentions and there's almost always a small group in front who stare at us, laugh, swear, and sometimes even spit in our direction.

They want to annoy us and they succeed; I just want to leave and never see them again.

Comfort always tells us to fight back, not to accept that they treat us so poorly. But she was born and raised in a country at war. For us, she is the rebel sister. When she came here she was thirteen, very thin, and she seldom smiled. It always seemed that something was gnawing at her. Even with me she was always so serious that it scared me.

Comfort can't stand the guys in the arcade and when they attack us, she gets angry and tells us to walk with our heads held high, and if we don't, she gets even angrier and tells us not to be cowardly and always ends up bickering with us.

Today we don't feel like strolling in front of the arcade, so after laying our bikes in the grass we sit on a bench in the park.

Unfortunately, after a little while we spot them coming from far away: it's them, the usual hicks, all dressed the same, in wife beaters with shaved heads. Today it's hot and they're not wearing the usual black bomber jackets with the Italian flag on the left sleeve.

This time they don't start spitting at us; instead they maintain their distance and start throwing rocks at us. I'm scared that they'll hit me. I get up right away and I'd like to jump on my bike to leave as soon as possible but Comfort doesn't want to go. She gets up too, and I get worried when I see that she's heading toward them. Then she stops, as though she wants to protect us with her body from the stones that those bastards are throwing. It seems as if the stones just slide right off her, and they're not hurting her at all.

Comfort seems so courageous to me, so strong, and I can't stop watching her. And all of a sudden I see her crouch down and take some rocks in her hands and then I get it.

"Comfort, what are you doing? Come on, let's go. Let's go!"

"No, we're not running away. If they throw small stones at us, we're gonna throw big ones at them. Don't you see that they're frightened? We shouldn't be. We shouldn't run away. Now I'll show you how it's done."

And she picks up the biggest stones she can find. Then she gets even closer to the guys and she starts throwing them; Maria starts to do the same. But Maria isn't as strong and I'm not even able to throw a little rock. The arcade guys are surprised. Maybe they weren't expecting it; they run away.

"She's crazy! Let's get outta here! (*Annamosene*!)"

Me and my sisters leave too. We take our bicycles and we start heading home. We also feel like laughing thinking about those guys' faces, but I laugh a little less than the two of them because Comfort teases me all the time because I'm always the same coward who only knows how to run away. And then she says, "But what do they know, sis, about where I come from? Next time they'll think twice about throwing rocks at us."

We arrive home all covered in dirt and with pebbles in our shoes.

Mom takes one look at us and tells us to go wash up.

While I get clean, I think I'm going to like having a warrior sister, but I would like to know more about her.

I would like to know what she used to do in Liberia, if she missed our mom, and what our grandparents were like.

I would like to know the colors, scents, and sounds of Liberia, but Comfort is a little bit like Dad; she doesn't talk about that country with us, and I just have to wait to hear something more from her or to go see it with my own eyes one day.

16
The Sound of Drums

Toom. Toom. Toom.

There it is again.

Toom. Toom. Toom.

I can't get rid of it.

Toom. Toom. Toom.

No other 15-year-old girl has this happen to them; only I can hear them.

Toom. Toom. Toom.

Drums. A constant sound, rhythmic, wherever I am it's there, following me. Or leading me.

I was eight years old the first time I heard it. I didn't understand what it was; in the beginning it happened so rarely. It came in lightly and disappeared, delicate, passing from one ear to the other and then leaving me be.

I thought it depended on the fact that my father listened to so much music at home; I thought that the rhythm stayed in my ears somewhere and without warning, popped back out.

Toom. Toom. Toom.

Then I got bigger and the sound got bigger with me. It got louder and louder and more frequent. I began to experience it as a fierce lure. There's something searching for me.

Maybe it's the sound of my homeland, still far away and unknown.

Toom. Toom. Toom.

I feel it and I become one with the sound—I am part of it—and the more I hear it the more my desire to follow it grows. What if it swept me away from myself, out of my own mind?

At times it seems to go nuts and I try ignoring it, but the more I ignore it the more it's present, almost violent. I can't do without it, or it can't do without me. If I ignore it, it gets stronger.

Sometimes other sounds accompany the drums. If I welcome them and let them join me, I recognize songs in an unknown language that I feel is mine, as if they were familiar.

I've never told any of my friends. How could I explain something like that without being considered crazy? I don't want to be branded as the one who hears voices.

I know it could be signs of being a medium, a conduit—my mother once told me about that—but it's not easy to accept.

One time when I was little I remember having a very high fever. In my nightmares I saw women dancing furiously around me, dressed in ethnic and traditional dresses and jewelry. I woke up in the dead of those nights to the sound of drums. I asked my father to make it stop. Dad said that soon I would learn to live with it just like my aunties and the women of his village.

Soon is now and I have to deal with it.

It's evening, I'm alone, in the dark, in front of the gate to the yard.

Toom. Toom. Toom.

This time the drums grow louder.

Toom. Toom. Toom.

Hundreds of them.

Toom. Toom. Toom.

It feels like they are beating on me; I hear them resonating deep in my body.

I have to cover my ears with my hands to defend myself from that deafening sound.

I freeze, close my eyes, and wait for it to finish. It can't last forever.

The sound slowly subsides and so does the tumult within me.

I open my eyes and I see it. It's a silhouette.

I gasp, close my eyes again, then open them again. I rub them and look one more time.

The silhouette is still there. I focus more and recognize it. It's my Grandmother Jessie, the mother of my mother. She's wearing a long red skirt with African patterns and a white top. I see her very clearly in the dark.

What are you doing here, Grandma Jessie?

I've never met her. I've only seen her in a photograph, the one in the living room in a silver frame. She died during the war. Why do I see her here in front of me?

I begin to think that it's a ghost, but I don't believe in ghosts.

Nevertheless, it's not real because it couldn't be. I just wish I could pass her by, enter the house, and forget about it. But then she begins to talk.

I don't hear the drums anymore, now that I hear her voice. She's speaking in *Grebo*, her language. She tells me to come close and not to be frightened. Then I back away, my legs trembling and I have no intention to go to her. But she insists and opens her arms as if to welcome me.

I back away even further and I tell her no. At that point she disappears. I wait, still trembling, then I slowly approach the front door and go inside, finally safe.

These apparitions continue into the following days, every time I pass the yard and I'm alone. I'm so frightened that I no longer want to leave the house; I don't want to see her.

I don't know what it is, nor what it wants from me; I'm just scared.

My parents ask what's happening to me; they see me changed and they don't understand why. And I can't take it anymore and I tell them about the drums, the same ones I used to hear when I was little, about Grandma, and about my fear of seeing her.

My father, with his ancient but also somewhat trivial wisdom, tells me, "Why are you scared of your grandmother? You shouldn't be frightened. Listen to what she's saying to you!"

Maybe he's right and there's no reason to be afraid. It's my grandmother; she can't hurt me.

Whatever would she want to say to me? And why me and not someone else in the family?

I've decided: I'm going to follow my father's advice.

It's night. I leave the house intentionally to find her.

I feel strong and the desire I have to confront this mysterious thing is strong. Grandma is part of my origins and I need to go back to my African roots to understand who I am and what my place is in this world.

I'm here. I want to listen to you. Talk to me.

I wait but Grandma doesn't appear.

No vision, no long red skirt swishing in front of me.

The drums don't beat anymore. They have paved a way for me but I'm not yet ready to follow it.

17
The Black Body

Passing by the arcade continues to be a problem.

Those hick boys are always there. It seems like they don't have anything better to do than size up people walking by, shout obscenities, and spit on me and my sisters.

And yet not all of the group behaves this badly. There's Yuri, for example, who always greets me with a smile. And he isn't only good-mannered. He is also handsome, with dark features, broad shoulders, and tight shirts that accentuate his chest. My sisters don't like him and Comfort says he's definitely an idiot.

But I think he's a super cool guy, and he doesn't call us names like the others. It seems like I'm not the only one who likes him because all the girls in town want to get with him. He zips around Grottarossa on his moped, looking all fly, but when we cross paths he slows down and sometimes he even winks at me. I go weak in the knees.

A few days ago, I bumped into him on the street. He stopped and asked me to go out with him. So, in a heartbeat, without even thinking about it, I said yes.

We agreed to meet at a newspaper kiosk near a gambling joint. I'm heading there now. As I near him, I see that he's waiting for me on his moped and he's hunkier than usual. I can't believe what's happening. I snap out of it and make my way toward him. He looks me up and down with a gaze that makes me feel more head over heels than before. He tells me to hop on his moped. We don't have helmets; nobody uses them. I just hope my sisters don't see me. I of course didn't tell them that I was going out with Yuri. I didn't want to listen to them call him a loser like they do his friends.

But what do they really know about him? What do they know about how it feels to be asked out by the coolest guy in town?

I wore pants, my new ones, because I thought he would whisk me around on his moped. He speeds off and drives like a lunatic. I hold on to him tight so I don't fall off but also because I like to wrap my arms around him. I bring my cheek to his back, near the nape of his neck, and I get a waft of his sweet scent.

We arrive at an abandoned farmhouse, where I have never been before, but I know that everyone goes there to get bombed. We get off the bike, and he takes one look at my face and asks me what's wrong. I don't want to complain in case he thinks less of me, but this place is a dump. I don't like it and I want to go somewhere else. I finally muster up the courage to tell him, but he convinces me to stay calm and replies, "Come on, let's go in. It's scary out here."

I decide to trust him, even if I would have preferred to sit together on a bench or at his house.

The ground is covered in rubble, broken tiles, and pieces of brick. The roof has partially collapsed and it's unbearably cold. I feel anxious and I want to leave, but Yuri holds me from behind and whispers in my ear, "Relax, I brought you here because I want to be alone with you."

Then he turns me around and kisses me, and I feel better. He immediately sticks his tongue in my mouth and it doesn't seem real that I'm here with him. And I no longer care that this place is gross; I only want him to keep kissing me. I close my eyes so I can imagine I'm somewhere else. I channel all of my feelings into the warm and wet tongue of that boy who wants me and only me.

He starts to move his hands all over my body. He lifts up my sweater and his white fingers trace my Black skin. He leans me against a wall and I feel the damp, peeling plaster against my back while Yuri's breath warms my ear as he whispers he wants to fuck me. I don't understand anything anymore, and I don't react when he unzips his jeans, takes it out, and starts to masturbate. Then he asks me to give him a blowjob, and as he talks, he pushes my head down with his hand. But then he rethinks things and we change positions. Now he leans his back against the broken wall and I'm in front of him. And again, he tries to make me kneel and pushes me toward the ground.

I don't feel like giving him a blowjob. It seems like he brought me here just for that and I want to tell him this, but I can't because then he might leave me and find another girl who will give him a blowjob. And we won't go out together anymore, and maybe it'll be my turn to be made fun of by my sisters if they find out.

And so I get on my knees. I'm uncomfortable because there are shards on the ground and I'm afraid I will cut myself. I hear him say *brava* as he strokes my hair like a dog. I continue doing it a bit, even though I don't want to keep going. I don't like what I'm doing. I'm not having fun so I pull away and start to get up—but it's too late. He cums on my face and lets out a laugh. I feel that sticky liquid on my skin and it disgusts me. I want to throw up, but I'm distracted by laughter coming from nearby.

I'm still on my knees smeared with filth and even though I'm ashamed, I lift my head up, turn around and look at them. They are the hicks from the arcade, his friends, the ones who pummel me with insults.

Suddenly I realize that they were there the whole time, hiding in the middle of all that junk, watching.

I try to make eye contact with Yuri, but it's as if I no longer exist. While he finishes putting his pants on, I hear him say, "So what did you think, that I like Blacks?" And I don't know if he's talking to me or if he already returned to his gang.

His smile seemed so sincere, and I believed him. But now he repulses me as I sit in the middle of the rubble with ten or more guys who make fun of me. And I'm scared. I want to stay here on the ground and never get up. Finally, they take off and Yuri goes with them.

He leaves me there, dirty and alone. But they're more disgusting than I am.

I hear their voices as they move farther away. I hear them talk about me. They call me "negra" and that word resounds throughout the empty farmhouse.

Then in silence, interrupted only by some fleeting sounds, the mice and I remain.

I wait a while, for how long I'm not sure. Then I find the strength to get up and dust myself off, at least a little bit, so that I don't have to return home and answer everyone's questions.

I have to walk a long way and I do it without thinking. It's as if my mind is empty. I only want to shower, even if all the filth will never wash away with water and soap.

18
Pidgin English

My father works all day and returns late in the afternoon. When he gets home, he's clearly tired and the first thing he wants to do is take a shower and wash away the weight of the day and all the dirt that peppers his jet-black afro hair.

After a shower, the only thing he wants is a plate of rice and to listen to his music.

Dad usually keeps to himself, but when he talks it seems like he was born and raised in the outskirts of this city. We speak different languages in our family depending on what we want to say. Mom almost always speaks in English when she tells us something or asks us about school. But when she gets angry, she breaks into her Liberian pidgin English, and it's enough for us daughters to understand she's mad. As soon as she utters a few words, we know we're going to be scolded. Sometimes she tries to speak in Italian, but she stumbles over her words, especially when pronouncing words with double consonants, which are definitely not her forte. Eventually she starts to mix her Italian with pidgin, which is often pretty funny, and my sister and I make fun of her a little. We have gotten into the habit of noting on the kitchen calendar the words she gets wrong in Italian or the ones she makes up.

Mom never speaks *romanaccio*, a dialect spoken in Rome. She says that Dad mustn't speak it either and that all the words he knows he brings home from work. But when she says this, she does so with a half-smile and I suspect that she kind of likes to hear him talk this way.

My sister and I have to speak Italian at home. Otherwise we speak in pidgin, which is more or less the family language because it's more intimate. When we're out and about, we use the same expressions our friends use. But at home it's forbidden. Mom gets mad and Dad isn't a fan either.

Sure, Dad doesn't speak a lot, but when he does he knows just what to say and he's almost always right.

My dad is truly a unique character and my friends love him. Everybody likes that his smile is similar to Eddie Murphy's and that he listens to music.

But as is always the case, when we meet other people's parents we see the best sides of them, the fun sides. So the moms and dads of our friends often seem better than our own. My friends call my dad "the wise one" and sometimes I think the only reason they come to see me is so they can spend time with him and ask him a ton of questions.

In reality, Dad talks more with them than with his own daughters. And sometimes I find out certain things about his life or his tastes because I listen to him talk about himself with my friends.

If he wants to say something to his daughters, he uses music. It's his way of communicating with us. He chooses a song and has us listen to it, but it would be more accurate to say that sometimes he subjects us to it, like the time my sisters and I returned home at four in the morning instead of at midnight, like we agreed. We slipped our shoes off at the front door so as not to wake our parents with the sound of our high heels. I opened the door as quietly as possible and we entered on our tippy toes, without even turning on the light. In the reflection of the streetlights that shown through the window, we spotted him sitting on the couch, in the dark. His big white eyes stood out in the darkness. When I turned on the light, because he clearly already caught us, I saw his finger resting on the stereo. He didn't say a word, he only blasted the music at maximum volume. "Faccio i conti con te" [I put up with you] by Luca Carboni—he made us listen to this song for six hours. We didn't sleep a wink. And from then on we no longer returned home so late.

I don't even know where he got that CD. Maybe a fellow worker from the construction site gave it to him. He probably had it stashed away somewhere because he knew he would need it sooner or later.

Dad almost never listens to Italian music, only Zucchero, I ricchi e poveri, and Venditti because they are the first music groups he listened to when he came to Italy and maybe he learned some Italian words from their songs.

His favorite singers, however, are the South African Lucky Dube, as well as Bob Marley, Jimmy Cliff, and Alpha Blondy. Dad likes music that talks about Africa, and how Africa must grow. And he likes music that fights for what is fair for others.

On Sundays, he sits in front of the stereo with his beer and picks out a record, which he carefully cleans and places on the record player, an old Philips. Then he lowers the needle and the music resounds. I watch him get swept up in the melody. I see his thoughts begin to race as he loses himself in a world where nobody else can find him. I think his music is very dark. It makes him ruminate a lot, too much, about things that maybe he would like to forget.

19
Roma Nord

I'm eighteen and I've decided that the moment has come for me to find a job. I want to have my own money to spend or to save and maybe even help out my parents. Luckily, I find a job almost immediately, close to home, in a clothing store on Via Cassia. I've always liked clothes and I also think that I know a few things about them. I believe that all the time I spent with my African aunties or with Pola helped me acquire a special taste for clothing. I'm more courageous than my girlfriends when I get dressed; I'm not afraid to be daring with colors, unlike them.

At the store everyone's nice to me, both the owners and the other people who work there. It's a big place and there's always a lot to do, but it doesn't scare me. I want to make a good impression.

I work the whole week, from Mondays to Sundays, and I don't stand still for a moment because there's always something to fix or a client to help. I also like to design the window displays or dress the mannequins.

But above all, I like to observe the clients. Sometimes I have to deal with ladies who are not easily satisfied and always ask me for something else to try on because they can't find anything that suits them. Or with a couple bickering because they have to go to a wedding but can't decide what to wear. Or with a mother who accompanies her son to buy shoes and, despite trying some things on, in the end she only buys something for him and nothing for herself. In just a few months many clients have grown fond of me. Some come every Saturday on purpose just to chat; sometimes they don't buy anything. There are a lot of people who have become my friends under the guise of shopping.

While they look for something to buy, passing from shirts to pants to shoes, they tell me what's happened to them during the week, how work is going, and all the news at home. Sometimes they spend hours here.

I listen to everyone. For me, everyone is important and I like that they specifically come looking for me.

One day while I'm fixing the shelves of shirts, a very elegant blonde lady comes in.

Right away I notice that she's scrutinizing me; it even annoys me a little and I think, "Why is she staring at me?" but without malice. In fact, I know that to some it still seems strange that a Black girl is a saleswoman.

She continues to look at me with a questioning face because I'm convinced that she thinks I'm someone else.

"You're Anna, right? Others had difficulty, but I was always able to tell you two apart, you and Maria! Speaking of which, how is your sister?"

This woman actually knows me, but I don't know who she is, and she's understood that I don't recognize her.

"I'm Carla, I was your Italian teacher in elementary school, Mrs. Carla. Don't you remember?"

She doesn't even wait for my answer and gushes forth like a raging river. She says that she's thought about us a lot over the years and mulled over what she should've done but didn't do and that she's sorry that she didn't treat us well.

"We put you through a lot when you were little and I'm sorry. Can you tell your sister that I'm sorry?"

I'm there slack-jawed, with the t-shirts that I should have folded still in my hands, frozen in the memories of those years and all that this woman didn't see happen or, if she did see it, preferred to ignore.

I snap out of my thoughts and look around: the store is filled with clients and I should be quickly putting away what people have left in the dressing rooms before someone else goes in.

But something blocks me again and I get sucked back into those memories.

I look at her somewhat aged face. About ten years have passed, not very many. I see the face of the woman who never defended us when the other children bullied us. She has a few lines around her eyes and she's dyed her hair blonde, she was a brunette before. Maybe it's easier to hide the gray regrowth that way.

I would like to say to her, "And what do you want now? Do you want me to tell you that nothing happened?"

But I remain silent a little longer. I wasn't raised to feel resentment or to get others in trouble.

Memories that I had set aside come back to me, all the times my sister and I hid at school, at recess, so that no one would find us and laugh at us. I remember my teachers and my classmates' faces. I remember them sticking out their tongues, eyes full of contempt.

In the end I'm able to speak.

"Miss Carla, we've also thought about you a lot, but there's no need to apologize. So much time has passed."

* * *

I would like to ask her so many questions, now that she's here in front of me, vulnerable.

I would like to ask her why me and Maria were separated in third grade, how they could have imagined how we felt, the two of us who have always done everything together. I would like to ask why they didn't realize how all the others treated us and how she didn't understand our loneliness.

But above all I would like to ask her if her thinking about us so much over the years really meant anything.

But it's not the right moment for all of this. And I don't even know if I want to go back to those days, risking reliving memories I can't compartmentalize.

So I ask the only questions I can ask, the most useful ones to put an end to something I really don't want to start.

"Miss Carla, how can I help you? Are you looking for something in particular?"

20
The 29

I've never liked waiting for the bus, especially not at the bus stops in Via di Grottarossa where there aren't any covered bus shelters with benches where you can sit and take refuge from the sun or rain—only yellow posts that don't make shade even for the blades of grass that sprout out from between the cobblestones.

Today I have to take the 29 to go downtown. There's only one every half hour and I hope it's not late because it's hot and the heat is oppressive and rather strange for mid-June.

I reached the bus stop with calm, early; I didn't want to risk sweating and thus staining the blush pink dress I'm wearing. I like this dress even if I think it might be a little too short, and for this very reason I decided to pair it with a simple pair of sneakers. Sandals would have been more appropriate given the temperature, but the fear of being too flashy pushed me toward a more sporty look. I don't want to attract too much attention.

It's the same old habit I have of weighing how others will see me, that sensation of always being judged. I never feel free to wear heels and miniskirts when I want to, and to simply *be* without feeling the gaze of others on me.

But even that little tweak isn't enough.

I've been there for a few minutes. I try to read some messages on my phone by raising the brightness on the screen, almost dazed by the sunlight at three in the afternoon. I see a police car pass by on the other side of the road, and from the way the officers look at me I understand they've noticed me. They stop, they put the car in reverse and after a U-turn, they approach me.

The officer in the driver's seat rolls down his window. I know it's not going to be easy to remain calm, but I have no intention of losing control. Dad always says that you have to respond with diplomacy to the powers that be, but a little irony doesn't hurt either. When I was little, they often stopped us to check our documents, and the policemen used to tell my father that his car was too nice and new to really belong to him. They always asked him so many questions, what his job was, how long he'd been in Italy, but above all they wanted to know why he lived in the Cassia district and how he got the money to buy that car.

The hoarse smoker's voice of the police officer brings me back to the present.

"What are you doing here?"

"What do people usually do at the bus stop? I'm waiting for the bus."

The officers talk a little to each other but, as much as I try, I can't hear what they're saying. The noises of passing cars that slow down to avoid them drown out their voices. The officer in the passenger seat leans toward me and asks for my documents.

As I grudgingly open my purse to reach for my wallet and pull out my ID, I notice his puzzled expression. I move slowly; I know I should be quicker so they don't think I have something to hide.

"Why do you need it?" I ask while I hold out my ID, holding it tighter than I should.

"Just checking."

I know they've mistaken me for a prostitute or for one of the girls at the immigration center; they're around at all hours of the day. It's hard to believe anyone would want to pick up a prostitute in this scalding heat.

"I was born in Italy; there's no need to check, and I know my rights. I know that you're only asking for my documents because I'm Black. Or do you ask to see the documents of all the white girls you see at bus stops?"

The voice in the background that comes from the steering wheel radio is superimposed on that of the policeman sitting at the wheel who, almost apologetically, says that there are many girls like me around.

"Sure. You saw a Black girl and you immediately thought that she was a prostitute. I just put on a shorter dress and it doesn't matter that it's summer, it's hot, or even that this is my neighborhood. In all these years, however, no policemen have ever stopped to check my documents at the bus stop."

The officer waits for a moment before telling me that their job forces them to do things they don't want to do, as if they were acting with no free will.

"Believe me, it's not about you. We do what we're asked to do, but underneath this uniform we are different people in real life."

In the distance I see that the 29 is coming. They realize it too. They put the steering wheel in motion, I take my ID back, and I begin to move away.

I touch my tresses: the sun has warmed my hair and it's almost burning.

I notice a patch under my left armpit; my efforts have been useless, but who knows if it's because of the heat. I sense that the policemen have not left yet, so I stop and look at them again.

"I don't view *you* in any particular way. Next time don't stop and ask a girl for her documents just because she's Black."

21
The Motivator

As we grow older, little by little the differences between my sister and I become more pronounced. And it isn't really because her body is covered in tattoos and mine isn't or because she shaves her head and I still wear braids. Rather, it's because we have distinct personalities. I'm as shy as ever and she's a social butterfly. Yet people still can't tell us apart, even if we don't look the same like we did in the past. Since we've grown up, we no longer do everything together. Maria has many friends, most of them guys, and for this reason Dad sometimes calls her Mario—the son he would've liked to have.

Maria is always out and about, and wherever she goes, she meets somebody who she introduces to us, even if she has no desire for a serious romantic relationship. She seems to value her freedom more than anything else.

For some time now, my sister has been meeting up with a group in Villa Borghese. Comfort and I often tag along too. The majority of the people in the group are of the second generation, children born in Italy to immigrant parents, like us. The group is also made up of the children of mixed couples, as well as those who arrived in Italy some time ago with their families. One of the members is named Samantha. She has an Italian mother and a Senegalese father. But she never sees her father because he returned to Africa when she was six years old, which is why she is so sad and blames her mother for separating them. She is my best friend and, if it weren't for Maria, I might've never met Samantha. Maria is like that, always working hard to help others. The group calls her the motivator because she doesn't leave anybody behind, and she has nice words and thoughts for everyone. She organizes and advocates without forgetting a single person, not even the friends of friends. There are also white Italian guys and girls in our group, all of whom love R&B and hip-hop. But most of the group members are Black.

I've never been with a Black guy, even if Samantha says that at least once in my life I need to go out with one. She has a soft spot for Nigerians and she tells me all about her sex life. Given that she's like a sister to me, I listen to everything she tells me. But when I make friends with an African, the first thing they ask me is if I have a white boyfriend. And if I were to tell them that I went out with white men, they'd feel I'd wronged an entire community. And yet it's not like this at all.

Time and again, they also ask me why I don't look for a Black man, seeing as I'm also Black—as if being with someone were more a matter of the skin than the heart.

We all go dancing together in the evening. As usual, Maria organized everything. It's Saturday and she convinced us to go to a new place. We are no longer fourteen years old and we don't have to go to the disco early in the evening.

We arrive in the Testaccio neighborhood. The venue is located below the stairs and it's packed with people; we are in the heart of Roman nightlife. The place where we're going is the only spot that is really Black and outside there is a long line. We have to wait a while before getting in, but once we're inside we lose ourselves in the warm, dim light and pounding music. We head down into the main area, which feels like being in a large cave with age-old walls.

There is a long counter and, behind it, there is a seemingly endless row of liquor bottles. There are three bartenders, and one is pretty cute. We exchange looks for a spell but then Maria arrives and tells me to either make a move or I might as well go dance, since that's what we're here for. When she sees me hesitate, she grabs me by the arm and drags me away. She has acted this way since we were little girls. She always seems to have the answer, especially when there's music in the mix.

I have just enough time to grab a drink before we hit the dance floor, along with everyone else in that jam-packed space. It's an unusual atmosphere; we are almost entirely surrounded by Black people, immersed in a reality parallel to the one where we live outside of this joint, except of course when we are together at Villa Borghese.

Comfort and Samantha join us on the dance floor; they never miss a chance to ask if I'm ready to get down. But Maria, who is always by my side and never gives up on me, replies that I only like white men.

Samantha notices a guy and, as she sips on her gin and tonic, points him out to me.

"Look how that brother looks at you. With that one you'd surely have three big sons!" The guy is on the other side of the room but realizes that we're talking about him. He makes his way toward us and pretends he doesn't notice anything. A moment later, I find him standing in front of me.

My sisters and friends suddenly disappear, but I know that Maria is watching me from afar while she makes sure that our friends are dancing and having fun, as if everyone's happiness were her responsibility.

The guy is about six feet tall and he is wearing a durag on his head, like Snoop Dogg. He stares me straight in the eyes with an intense look. It seems like he wants to communicate who-knows-what with his gaze. Without breaking eye contact, he grabs my hips and begins to move at my pace, as I surrender myself to the rhythm of the music. DJ Koko is at the turntables playing "Let's Talk About Sex" by Salt-N-Pepa. I think it might be a sign, and that the moment has arrived, as Samantha says, to stop talking about it and act.

I'd like to gently close my eyes to escape his penetrating and provocatory gaze. I'd like to be able to think freely, without having to listen to the opinions of my friends or Maria.

He moves even closer to me, and I feel something pressing against me. He does it on purpose to convey his intentions. But no, I'm not ready for that.

And all of a sudden Maria arrives. As always, she gets me out of that situation. She also senses that this hot guy isn't for me, at least for the moment.

22
The Guy from CasaPound

For a while now I've worked in a bar as a dancer on Friday nights.

The music is loud and the place is always crowded, but nonetheless I manage to zone out and focus on the movements of my body that follow the rhythm and sync with those of the other girls dancing alongside me. I try not to get distracted by the goings-on in the disco, like the guys who catcall me and try to make a move. I just switch places with a coworker and keep on dancing. During breaks, it's inevitable that somebody will approach me and ask where I'm from. Most people think I'm Brazilian or Cuban because they instinctively make assumptions based on the color of my skin and the fact that I work at one of those places. They ask me if I speak Italian and when I tell them that I don't only speak it but *I am* Italian of Liberian origins, they often respond that they don't know where Liberia is. Some say that I'm Liberian like George Weah, the soccer player from Milan. Others, however, can't see beyond the color of my skin and at most I hear them say, "But look how beautiful that *negretta* is," as if I were a slightly exotic object that adds a touch of color to the scene. I am never attracted to any of these guys.

I know very well that it won't be in that bar where I'll find love. Nevertheless, as of late there are a pair of eyes amidst that disorderly crowd that watch me like nobody has ever done before. That gaze belongs to a guy who sits at a table by the stage every Friday with his friends.

I see him whisper something into the ear of another guy. I continue dancing. I take a step and spin around when I feel something brush my ankle. It's him. I bend down to hear what he has to say. He just wants to know my name, he claims. He doesn't have the attitude of your typical pain-in-the-ass man. His eyes are fixated on mine, as if he wanted to capture my thoughts.

I don't even have time to respond before security quickly shows up. They are super jacked men dressed from head to toe in black who serve as our bodyguards. Usually they aren't very nice if they suspect someone is bothering us. So they ask me if he is annoying me and if they need to take care of the situation. I would feel bad if they kicked him out. He doesn't seem like one of the usual types who is rude and hovers around me. No, this guy has a gentle way about him.

"It's okay, he's a friend of mine," I tell the men. And when they're no longer nearby, I turn to him. "Listen, don't upset them, those guys. Now leave me alone and when I get off of work we can talk."

"I'm not worried about them. I only want to talk with you. I'll wait."

The night continues. His eyes are pretty much only on me.

At the end of the night, I exit the stage and head toward the dressing rooms. The security guards are ushering people out and they also tell him that he has to go. I had promised him that we would talk so I intervene: "He's a friend of mine. I will say hi and then he'll leave right away."

We are left alone in front of the dressing rooms.

"I'm Marco. I've been watching you for weeks and not only how you dance. There's something different about you that I like. Will you tell me your name?"

"Anna."

"Finally! Listen, before that bouncer comes back and kicks me out, can I ask for your number? I'd like to invite you out for a drink or dinner and to chat a bit, if you are up for it."

I give him my number, perhaps a bit too quickly.

"I'll text you soon," he says, and then leaves.

When I get home, I'm too tired to think about anything and I immediately go to bed. But when I wake up, I see that he has already written to me on WhatsApp to tell me that it was a pleasure to meet me.

I take a peek at his profile. His photo isn't particularly attractive, but a quote he includes strikes me: "Fighting is a matter of destiny." Before I respond to him, a sixth sense tells me to go and search where he got it from. It's a song by the group ZetaZeroAlfa, the official band of CasaPound Italia.

"But do you listen to ZetaZeroAlfa?"

"Why? Well, not anymore. Now I'm back listening to Liam Gallagher."

"I'm sorry, but I don't go out with extremists. You can keep eyeing me from below the stage."

"I'm not what you think I am. Let me get to know you and you'll see. For two years now I've been doing life alone. I worked for CasaPound for nine years, but things are different now. I'm different. If you don't want to go out with me I understand, but at least give me the opportunity to meet you and I'll explain everything."

I don't know how to respond. My mom's words echo in my mind—all the times she told me not to judge others, not even Italians who, as it happens, take for granted what they have and don't always understand their own actions.

"They have everything but they're never happy. The more love you give them, the more love comes back to you."

We meet at a bar in Trastevere. I feel all eyes on me. Surely everyone is wondering what a Black girl is doing with a right-wing extremist, as if it were written all over the wall. As if his political militancy were evident to everyone, like the color of one's skin.

An overbearing voice replays in my ear.

You went out with someone from CasaPound?

What happened to all of your activism?

Did you forget that you're second generation?

What happened to your interest in *jus soli*?

Remember that fighting is a destiny, even for you.

Don't forget about the murder of Samb Modou, Diop Mor, and Idy Diene in Florence. Or Soumaila Sacko in Calabria.

I want to leave. My head is spinning with all those thoughts. I'm there when he asks me, "Is everything okay? Listen, do you mind telling me why you didn't want to go out with me?"

"To tell you the truth, I'm now asking myself why I went out with you. I can't believe I'm at dinner with an extremist. Me!"

"Is this the reason why you didn't want to go out with me? Because of my past?"

"Because of your past and my present. I'm a daughter of immigrants and, even if I was born here, I'm also an immigrant. It's a constant struggle for us. You all have an issue with immigrants, migrants, and with everyone you think is different than you."

“It’s true, I made a mistake. But immigrants have nothing to do with it. I was a part of something, it was like a family, and I was willing to do anything for them. I was even arrested a couple of times, and now I can’t go to the stadium anymore. I believed in it, but now I’m only interested in my future.”

“And what made you change your mind?”

“Two years ago I came to the realization that I was only a pawn. And so I started to think with my head. I wanted to get to know people for who they are and not for the label we assign to them.”

“So God exists after all!”

We start to laugh.

“And now I want to get to know you. I like you so much.”

Something tells me he’s sincere and, as if washed away by a wave, I don’t let his militant past interrupt a moment of tenderness and understanding. We keep on talking, and when we leave the bar, he kisses me and I respond to his kiss as if we had known each other forever. I ask him if it’s his first time.

He distances himself from my lips, stunned.

“First time doing what?”

“The first time you’ve kissed a Black girl.”

But his response is lost in the thundering of drums. Never had I heard them so forceful and deafening. Those drums hadn’t visited me for a long time. Is it because I’m so confident now?

I move away from him and take a step back. The sound of drums softens, but when I try to get close again, it grows more intense.

My evening with him ends there. I can’t go any further.

I decide to give it another try, uncertain of the importance of the past and prospects for the future.

My past is a part of me, and his is a part of him. Can one really bring such an important past to a close?

We meet a second time. We have a drink and then he brings me home. I invite him up.

We kiss, an intense kiss, but I feel an immense wall between us, a wall that divides us. The more we try to embrace each other, the more I feel an alien world upon me. Once again, the drums inside me resound. At the center of my body, from somewhere, my world is speaking to me. I must distance myself from that boy; I must push him away in the name of peace.

What would my sisters and our friends from Villa Borghese say if they knew I was here with him? Even if he claims to no longer be the man he was before, there's something about him that makes me uneasy. Nine years are a lot.

I wonder what made him change his mind. It seems like it must have been a miracle from what he told me, a sudden flash of illumination that made him go from vehemently despising immigrants to wanting to go out with a negra, as they call us. He admitted to making a mistake, but something still doesn't convince me. How is it possible to change in such a radical way?

But nonetheless, I have difficulty believing that *he*, with those eyes, was one of those who yells "Italians first," one of those who protests against jus soli. Maybe he doesn't realize what it means to spend your life without being acknowledged, without truly belonging, with a residency permit that identifies you as a citizen of a country in which you've never actually set foot. He doesn't know what it means to be a foreigner in one's own country. I feel so much anger, which I express to him. He remains silent.

What scares me the most is the fact that he considered that reality his family.

How could a reality wrought with hate be a family?

And then, what might he have done to get arrested twice and slapped with a DASPO, banning him from sporting events so as to prevent violence? Who was he?

Was he putting on an act with me?

I ask him a few other questions and, from the few things he says, I understand he isn't a saint. If he could unleash his anger on someone, he would choose an immigrant. He tells me about the world in which he lives, in which he grew up, in which he was always immersed, a wonderful life in some ways but also a difficult one. He tells me about the wars between impoverished people that he witnesses every day.

I, on the other hand, long to tell him of all those times we went down to the piazza to demonstrate, to march against racism. But I don't respond; I think it's more important to listen to him. He is unhappy in his job and with his community. I look at him and see a fragile boy—but it's not enough.

"Excuse me, but you have to leave."

He stops to think a moment, as if he were waiting for my reaction, but he really just wanted to pause.

"Ok, I understand, I'll go. But know that our past is sometimes only a parenthesis that has nothing to do with us."

23
Fingerprints

For the first eighteen years of my life I stood in line with my parents in front of the police headquarters of Grottarossa. In addition to being under their guardianship, I also had their Liberian citizenship. Even though I was born in Italy, I had citizenship in a country where I'd never stepped foot, that I'd never seen except in photographs. Children of immigrants like me who are born in Italian territory do not automatically obtain citizenship there because, according to the law, we—the children of foreign immigrants—have to keep the citizenship of our parents. In Italy you get Italian citizenship by descent, by blood. I was just two years old when once if not twice a year we patiently waited our turn at the police station in Dad's arms. Fingerprints, photo, and verification of all documents, from my birth certificate to my parents' marriage certificate.

But now I'm of age and I have to do everything by myself. The police station has also changed.

When I open my eyes, the alarm is going off and it takes me a minute to understand why the window isn't letting in even a little bit of light. It's summer and as usual, when I get up in the morning it's already bright outside. But it's only five o'clock; that's why it's still dark. Like every year, the day has arrived when I have to go to the police headquarters to renew my residence permit.

I want to leave the house early to try and get a good place in line. I have to go to the immigration office of the police headquarters in Rebibbia and I know there will be many people and, regardless of the appointment I've made, there will be a long wait. I put on a light tracksuit because it's going to be hot, and I slip on comfortable shoes because I'll have to stand. I'm twenty-three now and the experience has taught me that the day will be long. I make sure that I have all the documents I need, and then I leave the house to take the subway. First I take the A train, then the B train, and then the 437 bus for Rebibbia. When I look around the bus, I mostly see people who are probably headed to the immigration office like me. It's like being in another world with its own rules and required documents and pieces of paper with the right lettering.

It takes a little over an hour to arrive and, as soon as I get off the bus, I see that there are already more than one hundred people in a line that snakes down Via Teofilo Patini. I slink through the barriers and find myself among immigrants, migrants, asylum seekers, embassy officials, and second-generation kids like me who feel out of place in this mix of humanity. A distracted eye sees no difference, but each of these people has a history, often difficult, and a future that doesn't always mesh with that history.

In my future, if everything goes okay, I'll have Italian citizenship and it could be the last time that I come here. My mother always tells me to have patience and I sure have no choice but to have it here in line under this beating July sun, squeezed together with so many strangers between the dirty wall and the barriers while we look at the sign of the immigration office above as though it were a mirage.

There are men, women, children who are crying, some who are sleeping, some who are attached to their mother's breast. Finally, after two hours they let us in one at a time. As soon as I'm inside, I see a purple tent and under it about twenty chairs. There aren't enough for everyone and they also seem broken; if I sit down on one, I'd risk finding myself on the floor. So I avoid the chairs, which are also filthy like the floor; I remain standing. At least here there's a little bit of shade. Who knows when they'll call me. I'm thirsty and I don't have anything to drink. I would like to use the bathroom but they only have the chemical ones and I really believe that the stench comes from there. I don't go. I prefer to hold it. I have to wait another two hours before they call me; then it's my turn. I pass through an entrance with guards who make sure that no one makes a scene. With this heat and all the waiting, someone might lose their mind. I pass through the metal detector and the safety check, then I quickly pick up all of my things and I head up to the first floor to have my fingerprints taken.

I run up the stairs. I can't wait to be done with all of it and go back home. As soon as I arrive at the top, a policeman tells me to sit and wait.

At least inside it's a little less hot, the chairs seem stable, and there's not that horrible smell.

I look around a little. In front of me there's the room where they take fingerprints and to see all of those police officers sitting in a circle, each one behind their own desk, makes me anxious. I fidget in my chair and keep looking around. There are those who wear uniforms and those who wear button-up lab coats, but more or less everyone makes jokes about the people who enter. They make fun of them for the way they wear their hair or for the surname they have, and if they don't speak Italian well they laugh and repeat the words that people mangle or pronounce with the wrong accent.

One policeman loudly says to the other, "Here's another one! What do you think his name is? He looks like Bruce Lee (*Eccone 'n altro! Questo come lo chiamano? Ao Sembra Bruce Lee*)."

Another yells even louder: "He's headed your way. You're in trouble now (*Sta a veni' da te. Cazzi tua mo'*)."

From the other side of the table another one says, "Spray it, spray it!" and a robust, dark-haired policewoman in her forties gets up. She takes out an air freshener and sprays it all over the room, waving it from side to side like a flag. In an instant, the scent of lavender reaches my nostrils. I hear the policewoman say, "Don't these people bathe? What a stench."

The officer stationed in front of the door finally calls my name. I approach him and he points out the official I have to go to: I get the policewoman at the table in the back of the room. I sit down in front of her; she still has the spray bottle in her hand. She puts it under the desk and without even looking at me asks for all of my documents. She glances through them quickly, and I know that this is a delicate moment. Just one wrong page and you have to start all over again. But instead she says to me, "Okay, everything's here. Let's take your fingerprints. Start with the index finger of your right hand and put your finger on the scanner."

In a pair of latex gloves that feel cold on such a hot day, she pushes my fingertips over the scanner, one at a time. When she gets to my ring finger I say, "You're not going to make any comments about me? Why don't you spray that air freshener? Don't I stink?"

The policewoman, with the face of someone who's been caught stealing, responds, "But what did you think I was doing? I was only freshening the room a little."

We go on to the left hand. I don't even notice what's happening in the room anymore. I hear noises, maybe other jokes and behind me I imagine the people going in and out and who knows if their documents are even in order.

Then I can't help myself and I ask another question: "How do you sleep at night? Is your conscience clear even though you think these people are animals? If I were you I'd feel like shit."

In a low voice the policewoman says to me, "Look, you misunderstood, Anna Mari'," but I tell her that I've been here the whole time, that I've seen everything, and I conclude with the words of my father: "Look, I'm Black. I'm not stupid."

24
Federico

It was James, a Roman of Cape Verdean origins, who introduced me to Federico during a moment of my life when I felt I needed to expand my musical horizons a little.

I wanted to become familiar with other styles since club music was starting to feel restrictive. I had already come into contact with Black music and admired James for his incredible rapping skills. I, on the other hand, couldn't come up with spectacular rhymes like his, no matter how hard I tried. He understood that I was looking for something new; he saw that I was trying to be the tough street girl, even if that wasn't exactly what I did best. The club scene was no longer enough for me, even though I had moved on to become a vocalist and had my own spot on a local radio station. But this wasn't enough either. I needed a producer to work on a new project and James introduced me to him.

He told me that Federico was a guy who knew a lot of musical styles, not just Black or electronic, and that he also had a passion for African music. James accompanied me to meet him and for me it was love at first sight, but not only because he was a cute guy. His living room was a recording studio, and I couldn't have been more comfortable in that environment. For me, home always meant music.

Microphones, instruments, vinyl records—so many vinyl records—like my father's.

We met to play music in his living room. We drank coffee during breaks. Sometimes I stayed with him for lunch and within a week we were already inseparable.

In the early days, Federico and I often wandered around the neighborhood, went to the market and to the shops near his house—always together, like all young couples in love. Federico loves to have breakfast in a café where his parents have been bringing him since he was little. It's a place with seventies decor; walking inside feels like stepping back in time. The managers are like family to him; he considers them uncles and he stops by every day to say hello to them. One morning he heads out early to their café for breakfast, but unlike usual, he doesn't come right back. He stays out much longer and I almost start to worry. When I hear him return, I go to see what's up: his face is dark, his eyebrows are furrowed, and he's pissed off.

Between serving one coffee and another at the counter, the "uncles" told him they learned he was seeing someone. They don't, however, tolerate such relationships, these mixed couples, Black and white people who get together. When Federico gets angry and tells them he will no longer have breakfast at their place, they try to make up for it by adding that they also have a nephew of their own who was with "one of these people."

His indignant words almost make me smile. When I told him about some episodes of racism that I or my kind suffered, he almost didn't believe it; he thought it was an exaggeration. But now he's experienced it too, and it wasn't long after we got together.

I tell Federico that he needs to get ready to see the world with different eyes.

My parents welcomed Federico in a very natural way, probably because he behaves almost like an African when we are with them. He's happy to listen to my father's music and to eat the food prepared by my mother, even when she serves extremely spicy dishes that make him turn all red. He particularly loves pepper soup, considered the regenerating food par excellence to be eaten when you're sick, but also comforting if you're sad or happy if you want to celebrate. It's a very flavorful dish that requires a long preparation and Federico shares these nuances of African life with us. He celebrates all the Liberian holidays that we do and comes to weddings, and not only is he congenial with others and others with him, but he has also become the DJ of these occasions and spins West African music; he knows all the parts and sings them too. No one sees his color; it doesn't matter that he's white. The kids call him uncle, my cousins are also his cousins, and since we've been together, he's been a part of our big African family.

This isn't a story between a white boy and a Black girl but between two people who love each other. I've already been with white guys, but they were very different situations. I often met them in clubs. They saw me dance and wanted to meet me, to have a different experience. I wasn't just a girl; I was a Black girl and they found me exotic and they wanted to go out with me. But when guys were interested in me regardless of my skin color, their families got in the way and pointed out what they really thought of me.

I remember Mario, a guy from Puglia. He always fought with his mother who would've liked him to date a girl from Puglia and did not fail to praise the qualities of other girls in my presence. When she talked with me she was nice, but she asked me if I get tanned during the summer, if I eat bananas, or what kind of food we eat in Africa, knowing very well that I was born in Rome. With Federico's family, I never had to go through that. I'm only Anna from Rome, with ancestors and traditions just like anyone else, and it mattered little that mine didn't coincide with theirs given that diversity is wealth.

At meals with Federico's father we talk about immigration and its political exploitation. He asks me questions about how I feel, what it's like to be born in Italy of African parents, but it's all to get to know me, to find out more, without morbid curiosity. I'm not an object to study; I'm a person to share things with. I don't have to prove anything to them. I don't have to be different from who I am or fear that they have accepted me on account of the color of my skin.

Not much time passes before I move into Federico's place. Here we can be together and make music and there's always a coming and going of people, friends, and musicians who knock at all hours of the day. It's a little like my childhood home: open, welcoming.

Here, for the first time I think about singing in pidgin English and not only in Italian.

Federico presses to organize a trip to Africa. He understood my greatest desire, my suffering, and immediately encourages me because he feels that my being African is present in the music we play together, but not completely, as if something were missing, a fundamental piece of me.

I sing while wearing African clothes, a turban. I speak of Africa even though I don't yet know who I am.

It's not always rainbows and butterflies between us because for those who weren't born into it, amidst the contradictions and difficulties of the daily life of second-generation children, however open, available, and in love they are, reality is a succession of surprises, many beautiful, and others complicated to manage. Sometimes it's not enough to want to succeed in doing so. Sometimes life is so complex that you feel overwhelmed and you need to understand even more, even better.

I know that Africa will be the answer to many questions, that it will direct me toward the future I want to build. I don't know what effect it will have on Federico and on us as a couple. But now there's no turning back.

25
I Dream of Water

Everyone in my family is afraid of water. It's an element that makes me feel uneasy. If I enter the water, I can't let go. I don't know how to swim or even float because I feel like I don't have that lightness, that confidence that would allow me to ease the tension a bit.

When I was attending middle school, there was a teacher who wanted to teach me to swim at all costs. I became a challenge for him. He tied the belt of a bathrobe around my waist and held onto me from the side of the pool while I tried to do some strokes, on my back or freestyle. He told me that even if really strong Black swimmers don't exist, it doesn't matter. I can do it anyway.

For years I asked myself why I couldn't really float, until I started to have those dreams.

They are agonizing, but I almost find myself anticipating them because I know that they are whispering something, a secret to be revealed.

They are dreams made of water and fear.

But fear of what?

I dream of finding myself in a river that drags me through its waters, and I flounder in the current, disappearing and then resurfacing.

I dream of being completely submerged in water, unable to find my way to the surface. I can't fathom how to get myself out of that river. Although with enough willpower I might reemerge, I can't do it.

But now there's no air left, and I'm searching for more. I need it, but it's never enough.

I feel my heart beat fast. I imagine it, ruby red, as it pumps blood through my entire body, blood rich in oxygen and life.

But then I am pulled under the water again, and a part of me is exhausted and lets go while another part fights to come to the surface.

I hear a loud noise in my ears, louder than my voice and, even if I screamed, the roar of the river would drown out my words, drown out my call for help.

In my dream, I ask myself how I ended up there, but then I remember that I was skipping from stone to stone, seeking to escape the water that I wouldn't know how to traverse because I am Black and there are no strong swimmers who are Black, my teacher always told me.

So swimming is for white people? But why then does the water beckon me?

Who knows if in my dream I went to the river to look for clay, to mix it with water and to play with that soft substance, perfect for shaping the world, my world.

I'm struggling to breathe as I descend deeper to the bottom. I'm about to touch earth at any moment. Yet it feels like an eternity that arrived too soon and now I don't know how to embrace it.

I try to reach the embankment but something from below pulls me under. And for a mere moment, my face emerges and I'm ready to scream for help but my throat and body are stuck. I continue to wrestle with the river but water quickly fills my lungs.

Suddenly I awake, gasping for air and lucidity. The sensations I felt during the dream slowly dissipate, as if they were threads of a spider's web that have entangled me. I reflect on my experience in the dream dimension and once again I feel torn in two.

Which of the two halves do I want to be?

Why can't I be both?

I feel as if up until now I have only lived on the surface of a time that has already passed me by. But now something entices me as if my body has been beckoned by the rushing river.

I am lying on the bed, my anguish has faded, and I relish the fresh morning air that drifts through the open window. The curtain ebbs and flows like a sail and it reminds me of the movements of the water, the waves of the sea into which I dive warily while keeping one eye on land to make sure I don't go too far.

But what if I had to try and distance myself?

What if the dream wants to convey that I need to let myself go, that I need to learn to swim in a stream of memories that don't belong to me but to which I belong?

Only I can decide if I should save myself or lose myself, and this awareness affords me moments of repose.

The parade before my eyes in the semi-darkness of the bedroom, the colorful clothes of my people, worn with pride and joy. Clothes that identify them and define them.

But what defines me?

I hear a distant dirge, music that recalls home and the past.

I remember that my mother spoke to me of her father, my grandfather Joseph. He didn't know how to swim either, but he had a canoe and sailed the waters of his land in search of fish. Who knows if he, my grandfather, was afraid of the ocean, or if he felt protected by one of the deities my people believe in.

My mother also spoke to me about them, aquatic deities, majestic yet feared, like Mami Wata, Mother Water. She's a fish woman, a mermaid who lives in the darkest parts, in a city of unimaginable beauty that can be accessed only through death.

Is it this abyss that was calling to me as I slumbered?

Must I somehow die, leave behind this life of white people that I did not choose but is nonetheless mine, and reunite myself with the deepest and most obscure side of myself?

My dream tells me that I need reassurance; I need to surrender to the water and let myself be carried toward what escapes me, my ancient roots.

In dreams everything seems possible, and then upon waking, I find only a sea of questions to which I still don't know how to respond. But I know that I must tread onward; I must heed this cry that runs through me like water.

26
Silent on the Surface

The war in Liberia is over. Lately, the greatest obstacle to my trip to Africa has been the cost of tickets. And the few times I was able to set aside enough money to go, my residency permit expired or I had some problem with my documents and wasn't allowed to leave.

But Federico's dad offered to give us all of his Sky High points so that I could fulfill my dream. With those points, we were able to afford round-trip tickets in business class, seats with all the bells and whistles. Federico's dad flies a lot for work, but he also likes to travel in his free time. I feel a bit bad that he's giving us his points.

I talked about it for a long time with Federico and, together, we decided to accept the gift. But something doesn't sit right with me. I feel as though my trip won't have the same spirit if I fly in luxury and comfort and I don't have to shell out a single euro.

This trip isn't merely a transfer from one country to the next undertaken for the sheer fun and adventure of travel. It's a return to my roots, and I'd wanted to foot the bill alone, without having to ask anyone for help.

Federico told me to consider his father's gesture for what it is: a gift. So we accept it and within a few days we plan our departure date. I don't have Italian citizenship yet, but I had my permit renewed. This time I will be able to leave the country. I will depart a Liberian.

Only one month left.

Every night since we decided to make the trip, I've been having a recurring dream. I'm in Liberia and I go to my father's village when, suddenly, I begin to run through the forest looking for my Grandma Gbonga. As I continue running, I'm afraid and I call out her name. I panic because I can't find her. My legs grow heavier and I lose strength. Although I keep running, my efforts are futile.

When I open my eyes, I feel uneasy in the wake of that dream. Federico tries to calm me down, but I know that it's only once we've started our travels that my anxiety will dissipate and transform into renewed consciousness. Now, however, I must wait patiently for these next days to pass.

One evening I tell my friend Edo about the dream. He is a film director and for a while now he has been passionate about documentaries. He thinks I should film myself every evening so I can talk about myself like one would in a diary. I have to discuss my state of mind and how I feel deep inside of me. I have to talk about the things I can't grasp when I'm awake, the things I have the courage to bring to the surface only when I'm asleep.

The trip that I have eagerly awaited is about to begin, and perhaps I'm not ready for it. Or rather, I am ready but I'm afraid of the unknown, of what I might find, or worse, what I'll never find.

Edo lends me a little video camera and a voice recorder. It's time to go to bed and I decide to try and sleep.

I shut myself in a room that we usually use as a storage space. There is a pullout couch there and I turn on a lamp that sits on a cabinet. It emits a soft, warm light that helps me relax my eyes and focus on my emotions.

I turn on the camera and point it toward me, but I instantly understand that filming myself makes me feel embarrassed. So I grab the recorder because I'm used to listening to the sound of my voice on audio. It's familiar to me and I like it. I hold it in my left hand and I start to talk about what I'm feeling, but a lump in my throat prevents my voice from sounding.

How is it possible that I, who sings my feelings to the world, can't seem to capture my most basic sentiments on that little gadget?

I alternate long silences with a few words. But even when I can't seem to squeeze out a single syllable, I let the recorder capture the absence of sound or my faint breathlessness.

Only on the surface am I silent. In reality, there is a mass of emotions about to explode.

And finally, my words find their way, in fits and starts, flowing like a reckless river that suddenly comes to a standstill.

Almost two hours have gone by. It's midnight and I feel exhausted. I need to find slumber, hoping I don't dream that I'm searching for my grandmother in the forest.

27
Mom Doesn't Want Me to Go to Liberia

The suitcases are almost ready to go; our departure is near.

You don't really think a dream will come true until the day comes when it finally does. You can't not believe in something; you can't not have a dream to make come true.

I think this is precisely the condition of those who emigrate and, when you are born to immigrant parents, you too learn to live it. To hope, to believe. And then believe, to see. Dreams in every moment, day and night and night and day, and then again the day after. A part of you is always closed up in that dream and—without realizing it—ten, fifteen, twenty years pass you by, waiting for something to happen.

There's a light in the eyes of dreamers; I've seen it in all those who pass through the Gehnyei house. I've seen it in men, women, and children. In some it had vanished. It happens mostly in those who pass through Libya, those whose eyes, more than anyone else's, cannot keep quiet. And then they too return to believing, and the light—that light—comes back. With the notes of Jimmy Cliff's "You Can Get It If You Really Want" and a beer fresh out of the fridge,

Dad is able to make them look toward the future. He was even able to do it with me, singing me the words to that song that talks about trying so much that you actually succeed. Dad played it so many times. Each time he put the song on, the house would fill up with faith in an instant because he fulfilled that dream. He didn't let it disappear.

The people who stayed at our house spoke to me a lot about Africa, about Liberia, about its political problems, about the absence of hospitals and schools, but also about its vast beauty, about the life that runs through it and the music that lives there. All of this fed my big dream for years, the dream of going to the land where I come from and where I've never been: Liberia.

"This little girl was born here. Why is she so curious about our country?" they would ask my dad.

"She dreams about it at night too," he would respond with a smug grin.

When you're small, you have a thousand desires that often change with time and they transform into something else. But mine have always remained the same.

And when a dream comes true, it lingers and you can feel it. It's just like the beginning of spring, which you can sense by its flowery perfume. You don't need a calendar, you don't need to know what day it is; it's enough to smell the air and spring is there, around the corner. And it's like that now for my dream. Its realization is so close that I feel like I'm walking through a field of lavender in bloom.

In the days leading up to our departure, I feel something digging inside of me. I don't understand what it's about; the only thing I can think to do is to let myself be whisked away by my senses. And so I embrace the same thoughts and emotions I already experienced many times in my life, in nightmares, in the deafening noise of the drums, in the dreamlike encounter with my ancestors and my land, that land where I will soon walk in real life, not only in my dreams. Maybe there I'll find that part of me that's still missing.

I feel that I would have been able to live a simpler life without constantly asking myself who I am and where I come from, but it was my ancestors who led me to this point, even if I don't know the reason why.

Perhaps dreams are in contact with ancient memories that our mind does not know and cannot explain. I don't know if I'm ready. And if these memories provoke pain?

Now that we're here, I don't feel calm at all. I, who have never been afraid before. Today, however, it's as if I had looked fear in the face. I don't know if it was mine or someone else's, but I welcomed it, I accepted it, and I even thanked it for manifesting itself, because being able to see it allowed me to make it disappear.

My fear manifested today at my parents' house. Who knows if it was fear who brought me here, the fear of making a mistake, of not being able to do the right thing.

Now it's night. In the quiet of the house, I take a moment to record what happened, as Edo suggested. I take the recorder and I close myself up in my little room that has now become my shelter. I slowly return to this afternoon when I spoke with my mother.

I had never seen her so tense, so worried. I saw that her body was rigid with fear and that fear was transmitted to me too and even now, hours later, even just thinking about it, I find myself feeling that tension again. I would like to cry but the tears don't flow. Perhaps they too are petrified, so I try to use words. I place the tape recorder in front of my mouth and let the river of sensations run into it.

My throat is tense. My voice comes out choked, but as I speak I feel that the skein is unraveling.

Today I wasn't afraid of my mother but of what was frightening her. I clearly perceived the fear of a mother who does not want something awful to afflict her daughter.

Federico and I stopped by my parents' house to say goodbye and to pick up a few things before our departure. Over the course of the years, Mom accumulated clothes and shoes for little boys and girls and kept them aside, certain that sooner or later someone would go to Liberia. She used to tell friends, neighbors, and colleagues not to throw away t-shirts and shorts. She collected everything, and, waiting for someone to deliver what she had saved, her home has almost become a warehouse.

Now all of those clothes have been stowed with care into bags and on the top of each one is the name of the little recipient.

We sat on the couch together, me and her, to go through our itinerary. Auntie Janet was in the kitchen preparing coconut sweets, and you could already smell the aroma while Dad and Federico chose some music on YouTube. And while a series of Afrobeat music videos played on the TV that took us to Nigeria or to our beloved Ghana, with their *kukere* and *azonto* dances and lots of black asses twerking wildly, my mother asked me almost point-blank: "Anna, have you heard from Auntie Diana?"

Diana is a woman with whom my mother has a very close bond, perhaps because they belong to the same ethnic group and she too is elegant and determined like all Grebo women;

she arrived in Italy a few years ago, but she often spends a few months in Liberia and, most of all, she can give us some advice.

"The first thing that you'll have to do once you've arrived in Liberia is to see her. Your Uncle Robert will come to get you at the airport. Remember to take a little something for him too. You know what he likes in any case; a shirt or a pair of shoes will make him happy."

She doesn't even take the time to catch her breath but continues: "Do you know what you will do in the following days? Dad set something up with Uncle Joe: they'll bring you to Grandma's in Kakata and then you'll go to Wongbai."

I show her the presents that I bought for Grandma at the mall. While I was there picking out what I would bring her, I imagined her like one of those women of a certain age who live in the village and wear bright dresses that come down over the knee.

"That should be her size, yes. So many years have passed since the last time I saw her, but I still remember her. I remember her stature, her eyes, her hands, and the light color of her skin. And all that hair! So much that she had to do two big plaits every time she did her hair. You have the same hair. Put these things in your suitcase too; you'll see that they'll fit her well."

Dad and Federico are all caught up in the videos they have chosen, contemporary pop music from West Africa. Sometimes the two of them seem very similar to me. Who would have ever thought I'd fall in love with a white guy who loves African music and that one day he would accompany me on the trip of my life, my first time in Liberia.

Dad chooses a new video, "Tonight" by Burna Boy, but then he's not concentrating so much on the music because he turns to me and reminds me of the money to bring to each relative that I'll meet.

"In the envelopes there's forty dollars each, except for Uncle Joe. In his envelope there's one hundred dollars; he'll know how to use it for the whole village of Wongbai. Make sure that everyone has an envelope. It's not a lot of money, but for those who live in the city it'll be enough to buy a twenty-five-pound bag of rice, at least."

I laid down on the couch with my face fixed on the ceiling while Mom continued to organize the donated clothes and envelopes of money. The scent of coconut filled the room.

With a sigh I gave voice to what I felt in my heart. "We have so many places to visit and so many people to meet in such a short time. But I would also like to go to Martuaken, your village."

Out of the corner of my eye I saw that my mother stopped short while putting something she was holding inside the suitcase. I looked at her. The expression on her face was indiscernible, with her contracted features and big eyes, as if something scary had materialized in the room all of a sudden.

"Where did you say that you'll go? To Martuaken?"

"Yes, we would like to go there too."

"Anna, please don't joke with me. I don't want you to go there."

"But why, Mom?"

"Because I told you that you can't go there; there's nothing else to discuss."

"Sorry, if I go to Dad's village, why can't I go to yours too? I want to see the place where you grew up."

"It's not like Wongbai. None of my relatives are there anymore. What would you go there to do?"

I tried to explain to her that I would like to see the places, the ones she told me about when I was little, with my own eyes. However, I wasn't able to tell her that I'd like to go there to say hello to my grandparents who aren't with us anymore but who once lived there. Grandpa died a few months after my mom arrived in Italy, while Grandma Jessie died of hunger during the war. She's appeared to me several times in my dreams, along with the sound of drums. Nobody knows where she's buried, but I hear that in Martuaken I could find something, something of hers, something of her.

I argued so much with Mom this afternoon that I couldn't resign myself to her "no." I also provoked her a bit, asking her if she was afraid that I might find out that everything she told me as a child was a fairy tale and in reality that wonderful village of her childhood never even existed.

But she didn't give in.

With a bitter tone and a hard expression that I had never seen before, she only said that I couldn't go there and that I wouldn't go there.

But I wasn't able to accept her "no" and she guessed that I would do as I pleased and not obey, because by that point nothing could stop me.

Our tone was loud and tense. Dad and Federico were looking at each other without saying anything while Auntie Janet came running from the kitchen, beckoned by our shouting. She embraced my mother, speaking to her in Grebo to calm her down and to prevent me from understanding what she was saying. Then she turned to me, still keeping her hands on Mom's shoulders and said, "Your mother is not angry with you, she's only worried. There are things that you can't understand, Anna."

"Liberia is your home; nothing will happen," said my dad.

But Mom's response was dry: "Your father has forgotten how much time it takes to get to Martuaken. It's very far from Wongbai, in the southernmost corner of Liberia and next to the Atlantic Ocean. One day is not enough to get there."

Auntie Janet had returned to the kitchen and I tried to cheer Mom up with a smile.

"We'll go by car; it's nothing you need to worry about."

"The roads are still in ruins and it will be difficult to get all the way there. But that's not what worries me. Knowing you, I know that you'll find a way to get there."

"So what's the problem, Mom?"

"We don't have enough money for everyone. And you can't go there empty-handed."

I know that it's just an excuse. Although I asked her more questions, she didn't want to tell me anything else.

I know that the issue of money is only an excuse. She's always said that for her family, money was never important, that they had always lived happily with very little. Mom went back to Liberia only once since she moved away. She went there to get Comfort and then she immediately left for Italy because the war could have started back up at any moment.

But that fear in her eyes, her outright prohibition, made me understand that there's more she's hiding from me, something big. Until this afternoon I believed that my overwhelming desire to go to the place where she grew up was also shared by her, that it was an obvious part of my dream. I try not to be selfish and not to insist any further.

I will not go to Martuaken.

28
The Journey to Liberia

Last night I hardly slept a wink. I tossed and turned in bed without falling asleep. Fortunately, my alarm clock went off early; I had set it for four in the morning, and I didn't have any problems getting up. Rather, it was a relief. Federico, on the other hand, looked very drowsy. Shortly after, we heard the doorbell ring. His mother picked us up to drive us to the airport. In the car we said very little. They both respect my silence because they understand that emotions tighten my throat.

At check-in, I let Federico figure everything out. He takes the tickets and speaks with the employee. When they ask for my documents, I get agitated as always. I have the label of an immigrant, and I'm not yet Italian in the eyes of the state.

Federico realizes this.

"Come on, try to relax! Aren't you happy? Don't you realize, love, that we're finally going to Africa? We're going to Liberia!"

He's right, but I'm having trouble focusing on what's happening.

We board the Air France plane and head to first class. It almost seems excessive to me, all of that luxury that doesn't vibe with my state of mind. Liberia is roots, family, stories that border on magic; it's home. I don't travel as a simple tourist.

Federico, on the other hand, is not bothered at all. On the contrary, he's as excited as a kid on a trampoline.

"Look at these seats, Anna! They're like beds! And there are even blankets!"

Then he points out the screen in front of us, on which the itinerary we will follow is traced: we will travel for twelve hours, making a stopover in Brussels.

The plane takes off. I'm next to the window and I look outside. I see that we're flying over the Italian coast and my eyes fill up with the blue and brown of the landscape. But it's the color of the sea—a pure blue—that attracts me more than anything and has the power to calm me down a bit.

Federico bought a new camera and he begins taking pictures of everything, myself included. Between one thing and another he kisses me, hoping to calm me down. When we look back at the shots he took, we notice that I'm never smiling.

"Give me a smile, come on! It looks like you're going to a funeral."

We begin to laugh. He's managed to get me out of my head a little.

When we land in Brussels, a man in a jacket and tie gets on, and he sits on the other side of the aisle from us. He's carrying a leather briefcase and, as he puts it down, I notice that his fingers are full of rings. I have no doubt that they're real diamonds, since they shine like the ones in the stories that my mom told me. And I ask myself what on earth he's going to do in Liberia. Maybe he's one of those white guys who traffic in blood diamonds, but maybe my imagination is running wild.

While we fly over the desert, the colors of Europe get farther and farther away and we begin to see the red earth of Africa.

I slowly drift into a deep sleep that I felt I needed but didn't dare give in to.

"Anna, wake up. We've arrived in Liberia," says Federico, delicately shaking my shoulder.

"What do you mean, arrived?"

"We've arrived. Look," and he points to the window.

With my eyes still heavy with sleep I move to the window and I see the Liberian coast. Shortly afterwards Monrovia appears below us, Roberts International Airport.

I feel the blood rapidly running through my veins, I feel like it's going to come out and I catch a glimpse of my arms: my veins are dark. The sound of drums is back. Something or someone is calling me but it doesn't have a voice. It's a whirlwind of sounds that prevent me from hearing everything else.

Federico's talking to me but I don't understand him. From the movement of his lips I intuit that he's prompting me to go: "Anna, we have to get off."

All eyes are on us once we deplane, or rather, on Federico, on his light skin, his blonde hair and his green eyes. We get lost right away. There aren't many directions posted, and the coming and going of people who are milling about make this place look like a metro station during rush hour or a particularly busy local market. After a bit, we find the conveyor belt with our suitcases, but there aren't any people waiting. It seems like they just take the first bag that they see.

Federico looks around and then I hear him yell: "Anna, run! There's our luggage; that guy has them, run!"

With the sound of drums in my ears, blood in my veins that flows even more quickly, I start running toward the man who Federico pointed out, dodging swarms of people and suitcases. I finally catch up to him.

"Sorry sir, this bag is mine!"

"Oh really?! Okay, take it."

The man holds out the bag to me with the same simplicity with which he was carrying it away.

I recover from the shock and Federico and I get in the line together with all the other people who are there, an endless queue of people waiting to have their bags checked. Behind us, there's a mom with two kids. They have loose, sporty clothes and the latest model of Air Jordans on their feet. I hear them talking and I understand that they're Afro-American because they're not using even one word of pidgin English.

After a very long wait, our turn finally comes. The security agent opens one of our bags, stares at Federico, and starts to talk with his colleague, in pidgin, thinking that we won't understand him.

"Where is this girl going with this white guy? And what are they doing with all of this children's clothing? Look at all this stuff!"

Despite the chaos and agitation, I feel at home. I can't resist and I show off my pidgin, saying that I'm Liberian and that all of those clothes are for the children in an orphanage. We only brought a couple sets of tracksuits for ourselves. The man stops to look at me and then at his co-worker, but before they can say anything I hear someone who's yelling my name.

"Is there an Anna Maria Gehnyei here? Her Uncle Robert Freeman is waiting for her outside. I've come to fetch you."

"She is here," says Federico right away.

The man comes up to me: "You're Anna?"

I can only nod. Only my family members call me that.

Then he tells the controller that I'm the niece of the Liberian-Italian and the agent turns to me and says, "Well, you could have told me that you're Robert Freeman's niece! Go ahead, but first tell me: where did you learn to speak pidgin Liberian so well?

"My parents taught me."

"They did a great job. Usually people who come back after so much time can't even speak a word of it. Americans, of course, only speak American and they don't bring anything for their people. Welcome home."

The eyes of the people near us are no longer fixed only on Federico but also on me, and about ten people compete to lead us toward the exit.

As soon as we're outside, the orange light of the sunset blinds me and I'm forced to close my eyes. When I open them, they focus on my Uncle Robert, there in front of me. I begin to scream and cry from happiness.

In a few moments, the sun sets and the city around us becomes dark.

I can hardly see anything, but I hear.

Music.

Music everywhere.

29
Oceanic Currents

When I see Uncle Robert, it's a bit like returning to childhood. Cradled in his bear hug, I am reminded of those arms that lifted Maria and I so effortlessly onto his shoulders when we were little girls.

He has always been somewhat of a mystery and a source of worry to us all. I was no more than a child the last time I saw him. I went to Sicily, to Porto Empedocle, with my father to attend Uncle Isacco's funeral.

There were many people at the funeral paying their respects to him, but they were mainly the people Uncle had helped over the years who were grateful to him. They outnumbered the relatives, a sea of faces I had never seen before but to whom I somehow felt connected, as if we were one big family. The good done by Uncle Isacco has not been forgotten and remains in the hearts of all those people.

Many of us wondered if Uncle Robert would join the funeral because there was never any way of knowing where to find him. When we suddenly saw him coming, it was clear he wouldn't have missed that moment for the world. But it wasn't long after that the police showed up and started asking for the documents of those in attendance. I suddenly found myself in the shoes of an interpreter, with the help of my father, because we were among the few who knew how to speak Italian. The policemen's questions caused somewhat of a stir. It was clear that they were looking for someone, but they also wanted to know what all those people were doing there. When they asked Uncle Robert for his documents, we suspected they were there for him. While he took his time, they turned to the others. One policeman asked a girl with a newborn wrapped in a sling on her back how she got there. She looked at me and my dad, and it seemed that she had only recently arrived in Italy. She asked me to translate what he had asked her and from her slightly distinct pidgin English I understood that she was Nigerian.

"He wants to know how you got here," I told her.

"By boat," was her response, with the "b" so stressed that it resounded throughout that tense silence.

A light wind swept across the funeral and we all started to laugh in unison, like Uncle Isacco would have done. He liked to laugh and he would have appreciated this girl's unintentional joke. Even Uncle Robert laughed with us, despite that deep down he probably didn't feel like it, well aware that something was about to end for him.

We translated for the policeman, but he didn't laugh and soon he lost interest in us and turned his full attention to Uncle Robert.

They checked his documents and took him away.

The day after, my father barely caught a glimpse of him through the fence that surrounds the center where they were holding him before repatriation.

The fact that he was the first person I met upon my arrival in Liberia helps me transition from my daily routine to my roots, the familiar to the unknown. He welcomes me in

Italian and his questions about Italy continue all the way to Diana's house, one of Mom's friends.

Uncle Robert would have liked to return to Rome, but it wasn't possible.

I brought him a pair of shoes, the kind he likes a lot. He takes them in his hands and then inspects and smells them. "A pair of Italian shoes, o," with that "o" at the end. It's one of the sounds that they usually add in Liberia, as well as "ya" or "menh," as it helps to convey the emotion of whoever is speaking. He, with that "o," wants to express cordiality and lightheartedness. But to make sure I understand that he appreciates the gift, he adds: "Wow, they are so beautiful!"

We say goodbye with the promise of seeing each other again, but because of the many things I want to do during my few days in Liberia, as well as the long distance from one place to another, it isn't possible.

With a feeling of familiarity in my heart, I find myself facing my first night in Africa. Right away, other than the sound of music, I notice that there are barely any lights. I can't see the surrounding houses, but I can sense their presence in the naked night that cradles us.

We are in Monrovia and we plan to make it to Kakata, in Margibi county where my father's brother, Uncle Joe, lives. Their mother lives there too. She's my paternal grandmother, Gbonga.

But it's already too late in the evening so we spend the night at my mom's friend's house, on the ocean, so close to the water that enormous creepy crabs are free to enter the house as they please, oblivious to the reality that they might be caught and cooked up for our next meal. At night, my emotions are amplified by the sound of the waves that seem to crash against the bedroom walls. In the morning, we awake with the longing to jump into the water that engulfed us throughout the night, but not even Federico, who trains in the pool every day, is able to swim against these ocean currents. We settle for some coconut plucked straight from the trees in front of the house, trees the children climb with surprising agility. Then my mother's friend makes sweet almond cakes of a flavor that can't be found in even the farthest lands.

Our stay is different from the typical tourist holiday that is spent in a resort, the kind of trip that can render tourists ignorant of the very country they are visiting. Yet our experience isn't at all similar to that of the locals, mainly because Federico is white, which immediately sets us apart as foreigners. My knowledge of Liberian pidgin English is a huge advantage. It helps me feel like I belong in this land. But the children's endless little requests for money, or the fact that for those of us with money in our pockets there is always food on the table while others struggle to eat, highlights all the distance between our world and theirs.

The next day we meet the person who will accompany us, by car, to our next destination of get-togethers and discovery. Our driver, Roland, takes us to Kakata to meet my uncle, who was the second person after my dad to leave the village. My uncle went away to study and become a doctor. For a long time now Grandma needs to be taken care of. It was my uncle who moved her from the village to his home where he looks after her with his sister. My father and his brother had lost contact with them as a consequence of distance and war, but when Uncle Robert returned to Liberia he looked for our relatives on our behalf. This allowed my father to reconnect with him, along with his other siblings, and to help out financially with the little he was able to offer so that our uncle from Kakata could buy himself a home.

I liked the idea of going to see the fruits of my father's sacrifice.

As soon as we set off, we realize immediately that the journey won't be easy. Roland is a good man, but he doesn't take much initiative. He just lets things happen without trying to control them, and this doesn't really reassure us. Not that the situation is easy. The police repeatedly stop us because of Federico, and it isn't to ask for documents but for money. They can't handle that a sister is with a white man, even if I'm wearing a lappa suit like other West African women. To them, however, I'm a rich Black woman who comes from Italy and is married to a white man. But the thing that makes them most angry is that I don't give in to their financial demands. It would've been much easier if I had just paid up, but to do so would feel unjust, as if I were devaluing my own origins.

"I am also Liberian," I find myself saying. "My dad is Liberian, my mother is Liberian, and so were my grandparents. Even if I come from Italy, I am still Liberian!"

Soon a crowd of people forms who, listening to my words, start to shout at the police, telling them that I came here to reconnect with my family and that if they continue to behave like this then nobody will want to come. I look at them, I don't know them, yet there is truly a brotherhood between us, a bond that I haven't experienced anywhere else.

Could this be the belonging I always searched for but until now had been missing?

Paradoxically, the presence of those strangers makes me feel at home.

In order to avoid attracting more attention, the police let us go. It isn't easy to snake through the streets. Several times we come across demonstrations demanding an end to violence against women. Here, the government has seen their first female president in power. Her name is Ellen Johnson Sirleaf and she is known as "the iron lady." There are men, women, and children marching. There are many people. Their cries resound passionately and they are difficult to drown out.

We finally make it to my uncle's house, where Grandma Gbonga is expecting me.

I know very little about her. I was told that she is now blind and that she sleeps during the day because at night she is haunted by bad dreams. She has nightmares about the war and my Grandpa Gbaulo, who was captured by rebels and murdered in front of her eyes, a piercing pain that is impossible to forget.

When I arrive, I find her lying on a mattress on the ground. She is clad in an African-colored dress with a turban on her head. While she sleeps, I cry, overwhelmed by this long-awaited reunion. Auntie Nuai is also there, but like Grandma she doesn't speak English either. The only ones in the family who know another language, besides Kpelle, are my dad and Uncle Joe, who left the village to go study in the capital.

But our driver Roland is also of Kpelle ethnicity, and he helps by translating and staying close to me. He supports me when I'm overwhelmed with emotion and almost faint. My aunt informs Grandma, after they wake her up, "Your granddaughter is here," words she had been anticipating for a long time.

A few weeks before leaving, I had a recurring dream to which I wasn't able to attribute meaning. I dreamt of arriving in my father's village and looking for my grandmother. But I wasn't able to find her. I asked everyone but all that remained was a sense of emptiness. It was only in the wake of those dreams that I found out that Grandma was not well and that they thought she was about to die. They didn't think I would make it in time to see her.

When they announce my arrival to her, she begins to cry because she believes I have come this far to announce the death of my father. It's only after we calm her down and tell her that Dad is okay, and that I am there to get to know her, that she pulls herself together. She laughs, happy to have me by her side. She also laughs when she asks me who I'm with and I tell her a white man. She wants to give him a name and decides to call him *Nan kolè*, which means "white man." From that moment onward, Federico is referred to as Nan kolè. Now even he has a Kpelle name.

Those few hours spent with Grandma pass quickly and happily. And for her, they provide respite from nightmares. She turns to pray, and she blesses us, and she blesses me. I have a special place in the family that day. Everybody in the room is silent. Only the voice of my grandma resounds, a voice I had never heard before and that I find sweet and steadfast, a voice that transfixes everyone listening to her words. To me they are only atavistic sounds, translated by my uncle. And even if I don't know the precise meaning of her words, I understand that it is a significant moment. That woman who has lived so long invokes our ancestors, asks for their blessing, and implores that I have a prosperous life. As a child, I never received a hug from a grandma or grandpa. I don't know what it's like to breathe in their ancient scent when they hold you tight or to seek refuge in their arms. I don't know what it's like to scheme with them and play little jokes on my parents or to go to Grandma's house for afternoon snacks. But in that room I find pieces of what I was missing. I am finally a granddaughter and not only a daughter. My grandmother heard me and blessed me because she believes my wellbeing is precious.

I leave that house with a heavy heart, but the trip must go on.

From Kakata to Wongbai, my father's village, it takes around three hours by car. We depart early in the morning the day after so that we can spend as much time there as possible before we have to leave again by sunset. Visitors are not allowed to stay any longer in that land, because the inhabitants' beliefs do not allow it, and those beliefs must be respected.

The route we take can't be defined as a road. It's remote and difficult to navigate. And it only leads to Wongbai. I'm sitting in the backseat with Federico, who looks around with the sense of wonder and awe that one experiences as a child, or rather, in Africa. He captures everything with his video camera while I try to appeal to all the saints I know so that our journey goes smoothly and nothing happens to us.

We pass areas where poverty dictates time and space as a result of the recent war. But the rebels of times past haven't disappeared. Now they ask for alms on the street. For a while we are followed by two boys on a motocross bike. They ride beside us, looking inside our car, and then speed off. Roland doesn't notice anything when Uncle, who has talked nonstop, suddenly falls silent. A little while later, we see one of the two boys walking down the street. He signals to us to stop, and while our driver begins to slow down, I notice that the other boy is approaching with a machete. Uncle Joe also notices this and tells the driver, in a calm voice, to speed up, and he obeys. We didn't feel any sense of alarm in that car. Everything unfolded with the unwavering sense of composure that Uncle instilled in us. But the sight of the machete triggered memories of the civil war and the awareness that we are not in a film but in a real country still recovering from the scars of its recent past. We continue onward. First we find ourselves in the middle of a forest and then in more open spaces. Thereafter we arrive at a small market where we decide to stop. As soon as we get out of the car, everybody notices Federico and gets scared. Some begin to call him Jesus because of his blonde hair and sky-blue eyes. And news of Jesus's arrival spreads quickly. One little girl, who is four years old at most, wide-eyed and petrified, starts to cry uncontrollably, like the children of Italy's past who were scared of the Black man. But here, where the colors are reversed, it is the white man who scares her, even if he is harmless and smiling, a nan kolé who looks like Jesus and speaks *romano*.

"For once *you* are the immigrant," I tell him, grinning.

Among the market fare, we find a local delicacy, bamboo worms. They are cylindrical and yellow and still very alive inside those transparent baggies. Uncle wants me to buy some; they are rich in protein and apparently very tasty. But in order to try certain flavors, you must have been born there, in that food's home. I let Uncle buy the worms with the agreement that he will keep them in the glove compartment. He tries to tempt me by telling me he will prepare them fried or grilled, but he is unable to tempt my stubborn Western palate.

I knew that in my father's village they ate snake meat and in my mother's elephant meat, but nobody had ever mentioned these worms before.

The trip continues and Uncle Joe tells me about family, about his eight siblings, five boys and three girls. He tells me that when my father left the village, he brought the respect and affection of his parents and all the brothers and sisters with him. He tells me about how Grandpa was tortured by rebels until he died—details my father didn't even know about. His sacrifice served to protect the village that he presided over. He saved a community at the cost of his own life.

My uncle also sheds light on the meaning of our surname. Gehnyei, which means "he who is at peace everywhere and with everyone," is a name that speaks to the nature that surrounds us.

At a certain point along the way, I notice that close to where we pass by, there are forests filled with seemingly infinite trees. They are immensely tall and alternate with patches where it's clear they were cut down. I ask Uncle for an explanation, and he tells me that during the war the rebels cut them down because they thought that spirits flew freely from tree to tree carrying information to the villages, announcing the rebels' arrival to the locals. People were not the only victims of war, but those awe-inspiring trees also bear scars that only time can heal, just like the scars of men and women.

As the journey continues, I hear the sound of drums resounding inside of me. It isn't deafening, or alarming, but rather it's like the beat of a big heart, rhythmic and vital to life. I haven't felt this way in years. Maybe it's a sign. Maybe it's telling me I will find what I'm looking for.

We finally arrive in Wongbai, located in Bong County.

The road ends there and beyond it there is only forestland. I am about to get out, and I look around. I notice that there is nobody in sight and a strange silence pervades that remote corner of Africa. Even my internal drum has stopped. As soon as I open the door I begin to hear something. I hear the music getting closer. I hear song; I hear laughter. And I hear rain. Intense, crystalline, tropical. And the more it rains, the more the people move and stir and sing. Everyone surrounds me and I seek shelter. Out of habit, I think that rain should always be avoided and never embraced because it makes you wet. And then I feel rice. It's thrown at me as if I were a bride in a churchyard, and I don't know why they are doing this or what they are saying to me in that whirlwind of sounds and gestures that I don't understand. Federico also gets wet and we both have rice, straight from their rice plantations, plastered to our skin. A celebratory reception of rice.

Uncle Joe explains that when a new person enters the village and it begins to rain, it means that the person is bringing blessings to the village, and it's for this reason we sense all that excitement among the locals.

I make my way, following behind Uncle Joe. But the rain prevents me from seeing and I continue to wipe my eyes so as to capture some images of Wongbai and its inhabitants.

They were awaiting my arrival, I know it. Uncle or somebody else probably came to announce our arrival, out of respect. There are no telephones and one can only communicate in person.

I'm waiting to meet the two aunts who live here and have never left the village. And then I see one of them. I have no doubt that she's my relative. She's my twin; she is Maria. The resemblance is striking, even their mannerisms. Auntie Malò rejoices as my sister would, with that same vitality. She takes me in her arms and tells everyone that her daughter has arrived, hugging me and squeezing me and squealing with joy, singing her own style of rap, wiping away the grains of rice that are still on my face. She also has two daughters, twins, who are named Anna and Maria.

It's almost amazing.

Uncle tries to take control of the situation so that we don't waste time and wind up leaving without following through on all the things we set out to do. The fact that Uncle was able to leave the village to go study in the city, although he had permission, could have upset some spirits who were possibly summoned by the locals out of jealousy. He is adamant that he not enrage the spirits that appear after sunset. He also says it's important to leave before dusk in order to avoid excessive checkpoints because at night there is strange trafficking in those forests. We might become embroiled in a ploy with consequences that are difficult to manage. And given that on our way there Uncle, thanks to his composure, was able to pass the checkpoints without any issues, we know we can trust him. Traveling with a white man is a risk in those parts. You have to stick to the rules of people who know the lay of the land, as bizarre as their rules may seem.

First Uncle Joe decided to say hello to Grandma Gbonga's younger brothers who are still alive. There are four of us: me, my uncle, and Grandma's two brothers. We make our way through the village, talking, followed by a swarm of children to whom Uncle gives some spare change. They show me the huts built by Grandpa Gbaulo. They are made of clay and covered in dried leaves and branches. They look solid; they withstood the civil war. Then we head to Auntie Kapé's house, my father's other sister, the one who I haven't seen yet. She hugs me and starts to talk in Kpelle with the spirit of my grandpa, her father, to tell him how he should be so proud of me and how wonderful it would be if he were there in that very moment, given all the sacrifices he made during his lifetime. At that point, she brings me inside her house and takes her grandson in her arms, the son of her son. And then she passes him to me, telling me he is named after my father. Naming a newborn after someone is of great significance, and she is eager to convey this to me. Outside the door there is an awning where all the people who followed us sought refuge. I remain there with them while Auntie goes out into the rain and begins to dance barefoot. She dances for me and lets out a laugh. Then she stops and looks into the sky to talk to my grandpa while I try to etch this marvelous moment in my heart, that warm welcome that is more special than any other in the world.

But family is a place of mutual exchange, and I must also offer a contribution. My uncle, almost with the air of the head of the village, asks his sister Malò permission to hold one of her ten children—Anna—who shares my same name. One who gives their name to another is indeed responsible for them and must take care of them because it is someone who has made it. They seem to think I am successful, so now I must look after little Anna.

What will I do for her? Maybe I can help her leave the village or with her studies. It isn't clear. The only thing we know is that names create connection and Uncle emphasized this point through his actions.

While Auntie Kapé danced and everyone watched the two of us, entranced by those same movements that appeared in my dreams, Uncle Joe had one of my cousins bring Federico some *kola* so he could taste it. Kola is a reddish-purple color and it's part of the traditional spiritual practices in these parts. The nut is a symbol of life, as well as peace, and to offer it signifies giving life. Whoever welcomes a stranger by offering them this fruit is doing it in earnest.

When Federico takes the kola in his hand, a bit hesitant, everyone turns to watch him, even Auntie who was just dancing in the rain. Uncle Joe explains that when a stranger arrives, the people present him with the kola and say, "We are delighted you came to see us," and they wait until the new person breaks off at least a piece of the nut and eats it because this also means that he is happy to be with them for as long as he desires.

Federico accepts. He is glad to be there.

We also meet the village priest, and together with Uncle Joe and my grandmother's brothers, we congregate in a hut to talk about the future and the fact that Wongbai needs many things, including a school for the littlest ones. It's a reunion of men, and it's an honor to be the only woman invited to be with them. My uncle points out that this is the first time it has ever happened.

After we distributed the clothes we brought over from Italy, satisfied that every child got something, the village inhabitants give us a gift that conveys their well wishes for our future prosperity. They take a rooster and a hen, the size of Italy's geese and turkeys, and they give one to me and one to Federico. We have to hold them by the feet, alive. But I get scared because I don't know how to do it and the children begin to laugh and make fun of me. Meanwhile, Uncle has been frying up the worms and he offers them to everyone, including Federico, who is immediately at the center of that buzz of curiosity. Everyone wants to see if he will manage to eat one. He succeeds while I still can't bring myself to taste it.

The moment of farewell is less ceremonious than our arrival. It's as if everything went well and has already been said and done so now we can leave satisfied.

When we arrive at our destination, Roland asks me what I plan to do with all those things my relatives gave me. He opens the trunk and out juts the rooster and hen, huge and still breathing. There are also packs of rice, bananas, and many other delicacies from that land.

Auntie Diana's family, who is hosting us, welcomes our return with great relief. They had asked us not to go to Wongbai; it was too dangerous, they said, and so they prayed for us. But when they see all the gifts we received, they start to rejoice because they know that whatever comes from those lands is good, a gift from god.

The trip and all the many emotions of the day made me feel ineffably tired. But the family's expression of gratitude for all that food delights me. Nonetheless, the only thing I long to do is sleep. I'm aware that the following day the rooster and hen will be transformed into a tasty dish. I'm a little sorry about this because they are the first pets I've ever had.

Before drifting off into a deep slumber, I decide I can always adopt a crab.

30
Blessings

Music. Music everywhere, for hours and days.

In every place we visited there was somebody playing music, singing, or speaking with the rhythm of Liberians.

And then, silence.

Thunderous and thick, like a wall of fog that dulls your senses and obscures your surroundings, leaving only blurry memories in its wake. A silence that transforms the absence of sound into a screeching cry.

We are at Fiumicino Airport in Rome.

Federico's mom comes to pick us up, but we are barely able to speak.

An unspoken question unites us: and now?

We lived outside of time, in places where the clock doesn't dictate one's needs, whatever they may be. We had many commitments and things to do, but we always made time to admire a sunset or savor a new experience.

We are seated comfortably in the car where we alternate between speaking one at a time and sitting in stark silence. In Liberia we traveled in taxis shared with others, because the drivers filled their cars with as many people as possible.

They don't mind that they also transport chickens or enormous bags of rice. Everyone squeezes in and chats freely, even the animals, and sometimes everyone at the same time.

At the market, you hear endless singing, each soul with their own rhythm and style.

Now, on the road, there's only the sound of speeding cars trying to arrive at their destination at lightning speed as they heed the tick-tock of the clock.

Federico's mom keeps asking us about our trip. Maybe she thinks we are tired but that if she persists she can squeeze something out of us. She's really happy to see us, and she doesn't realize how difficult it is for us to live in this moment of transition from the "old" us and all that we have experienced while away. Even on the journey over to Liberia, I was subdued and assailed by scattered thoughts. I felt a sort of emptiness inside of me that I knew I had to fill. Now I am full of the experiences I have recently embraced, so full that there's no longer enough room for a simple courtesy conversation.

All that I'm able to say is that Federico was given a Kpelle name. And she, with the instinct of a parent, reads into my words. She processes the limited data that she has at hand and intuits that, for her son, his return is not merely a transition from Africa to Europe: the fracture runs much deeper.

Federico's mom replies that he already has a name and her reaction, almost of annoyance, estranges us even more.

When we arrive home, we don't feel like unpacking, taking a shower, or settling back into our normal spaces and daily routine, or rather, our Western life.

We slump on the couch and stare into the void.

I reflect back on all the people I met during my brief time in Africa. And there is one person, outside of my family and my father's village, who has remained in my heart.

One day I accompanied a young cousin of mine to the hospital in the capital city because she had very bad dermatitis. The hospital was roofless, under the open sky, and music filled the air, as if we were at a disco. The songs were resounding from the national radio and, while I was there, among the many songs that played, I recognized one of them. It was a song my father played when I was little, a Liberian song called "Keep on Trying." I told Roland about it and he, to my great surprise, told me that the songwriter was a Liberian singer from the '70s. He was called Zack and during the '80s he was part of a duo, Zack and Geebah. Everyone thought he was dead, but really he became a priest. If I wanted, he would introduce me to him. And the day after, Roland brought me to his house.

The pleasure of meeting this man was profound and he was ever so grateful to me. He couldn't believe that somebody who came from Italy knew one of his songs and wanted to meet him. Once again, I met a person who decided right away, and without delay, to pray for me and bless me. But I was really touched by his willingness to give me the last record he owned. He only had that one because during the war they all vanished.

I brought the record home with me and now it's waiting to come out of my suitcase and find a special spot among my other music. But now, in this present moment, it's too quiet. If I close my eyes, faces and scenes, mostly of children, flash before me.

Children who dance through the streets for no apparent reason. Children from the village to whom I distributed clothes that Mom had collected via word of mouth and then organized according to gender and age. Federico's mom also collected many clothing items. Both of our mothers were eager for them to arrive in Liberia, where we also brought some to the orphanages.

We will have time to look at the videos made and music recorded, but for the moment it's enough to feel it all inside of us.

Roland also wanted to contribute something. He brought us to the village where he grew up. The village was peppered with caves and it was unfathomable how anyone could live there. Yet it was teeming with life too, a lot of it, and naturally music as well. Within a few minutes, a group of guys put on a concert for us, a party with microphones and speakers. It was an exclusive performance. Then they gave us some music to bring back to Italy so that it might be produced one day.

In the days following my return home, when I was finally able to cast off the debilitating sense of listlessness that seized me, I head to my parents' house and recount as much as I can about my trip, about Grandma, the aunts and uncles, the village. I tell them about Monrovia, Zack, the music, the ocean, the food, and the children.

I also tell them about Mom's two cousins who live in the capital. Visiting her village was unthinkable because it's even more dangerous than making the trip to Wongbai, as everyone seems to say.

I give her the manioc and peanuts that I bought her. I tell her how, at the airport, after checking my bags and finding these few items, they wanted to make me pay a hundred dollars to keep them. I also tell her that I had a breakdown. After being stopped countless times, after dressing in a way that would not attract attention, after abandoning comfortable outfits so that I would go unnoticed, after refusing to pay just because I was traveling with a white man and I myself was not born in Liberia, I couldn't take it anymore and I started to cry and release all the pain that corruption had caused me. While I've always gotten by thanks to speaking Liberian pidgin English, I've had to live with the feeling of being neither Italian nor Liberian.

Who was I then?

Who am I now?

I know that one way to unlock the answer is to make music. The urge to make music in Italy grows inside of me. I long to bring my roots and experiences to the heart of my work and life. I am moved to express all the warmth that trip sowed inside of me. At night I can't sleep—I write. My hands move as if guided by something mystical. During my days in Liberia, I absorbed many sensations that saturated me, and now I must release them into the world. I must give new life to my reunion with Grandma, the people of Wongbai, and the singing priest who invoked angels and archangels for me.

And in all of this, music is the unwavering leitmotif, an instrument with which I express myself. When I returned to Italy, silence enveloped me like a blank page. It's time for me to fill it, to unearth my identity as an Italian, to cease waiting for someone else to speak for me. It's time for me to advocate for those who don't yet have the voice I am now finding, the voice that I discovered while returning to my roots, and that I must learn to set free.

31
Italian Citizenship

I don't know what to wear today.

I had chosen some black pants and a jacket, but I don't want to put them on anymore because I don't feel like being fancy; it's not a special occasion. Rather, it is, but it shouldn't be, and that's why I don't care about arriving all dressed up as if I were going to receive an award or to be celebrated for being special. The reality is that I'm also in a bad mood although I shouldn't be. Today is a good day; today I will officially become an Italian citizen. But I've felt Italian since I was born. I went to school here, my friends are Italian, and my boyfriend, Federico, is Italian. To boot, Italian is my first language, I love pasta carbonara, and why is having Italian citizenship not my right as it is for all of the people with whom I went to school, with whom I work or go out?

The presence of my girlfriends grounds me, and their enthusiasm makes me emotional too and, in the end, I think that maybe this is really a great day.

No more interminable lines at the immigration office of this or that police headquarters.

No more residence permits.

No more statements.

Within a few hours I will be an Italian citizen—me, before all my family members.

Giulia and Simona insist that I dress elegantly. They want me to put on makeup and take videos of everything that happens to document the great day, they say.

A little while ago my mother called. She immediately perceived how I feel and she told me that all the troubles and everything they put me through aren't important. What's important is having made it to this day. Nobody from my family will be there because it's Monday and they're working. I'm sorry about that, but at least Federico will be there; he's been by my side through much of this journey.

He arrives here too and as soon as I'm ready we leave. We hop on the scooter and head to city hall.

I like when the air in Rome is crisp like this, on the cusp of winter. But really, I always like Rome because I'm Roman and there aren't any Romans who don't love their city.

When we enter the building the concierge tells us to go to the second floor. We ascend the big staircase and we find ourselves in an enormous, dark corridor. It seems deserted and we don't really know what to do. I decide to knock on an office door, but from inside they tell me to wait and that they'll call me.

Waiting. I've been waiting for a lifetime now; what will a few more minutes matter?

The room is full of paintings and antique furniture and the city counselor is behind a table. She's a middle-aged woman wearing a blue suit and the tricolor sash. I make my way toward her and my legs are trembling, but just a little bit.

The woman looks at me and asks: "Do you have your documents?"

I look at her questioningly because I don't know if she's kidding me, but she misunderstands and thinks that I haven't understood, so she starts speaking one word at a time while making strange gestures with her hands.

I turn toward Federico and my girlfriends to share with a simple glance the dismay at the fact that, even on the day of my oath, the person in front of me thinks I am a foreigner. From their faces, I see they're afraid I won't bite my tongue and I'll say something to the official, so I decide to stay quiet. I turn and hand the woman my ID. In response, I hear her say to me, "Sign here, *capito*? Sign in cursive. *Capito*?"

And at that point I can no longer resist.

"Look, I speak Italian. As you can see from my ID card, I was born in Rome."

I would like to add that she probably thinks that I'm a foreigner who's seeking Italian citizenship in order to get married and thus she's talking to me like that because she thinks I can't form a two-word sentence, but then everything fades because the most important moment finally arrives and only my voice can be heard in the room: "I swear to be loyal to the Republic and to follow the Constitution and the laws of the State."

The end.

The ceremony took less than five minutes.

Outside the building, far away from the official, I think the wait is truly over.

I almost get an empty feeling in my stomach. Maybe it's hunger because I didn't eat very much this morning or perhaps it's the tension melting away. I smile at my girlfriends who hug me and say goodbye because they have to return to work. I stay with Federico but all he does is fiddle on his cell phone, sending messages and taking calls. While we walk to get back to the scooter, I ask him who he's talking with but he's being all mysterious and just keeps smiling at me. He's so happy it's almost like he is the one who just got citizenship.

"No, nothing special, I'm just organizing tonight; maybe we can go get a beer with a few friends. Doesn't it seem like an occasion to celebrate? Let's go to the pub regardless."

"Listen, I don't feel like celebrating. You know that I didn't want to tell anyone besides Giulia and Simona because it's not a goal for me; it's just what always had to be."

And while I'm finishing this conversation I get a message on my cell: it's my friend Miriam who's congratulating me.

But who told her?

"It was you who told Miriam, right?" I ask Federico, who doesn't respond.

I keep at it because I want to know and he continues to tell me that we have to celebrate and we end up fighting, on today of all days when I'd just like to chill.

Then we calm down and Federico confesses that he was organizing a surprise party for me and he's invited all my friends. At this point I get even more angry, not because of the party but because I feel misunderstood. This is not a special day.

I don't know if it's difficult for him and all the others to comprehend, but for me, this is just the first day of normality.

32
Karima

The sound of drums is gone.

It no longer demands my attention and calls me back to my homeland; it no longer tells me that there's a part of me in a faraway place and that to be me, wholly, I have to fit the pieces together. That *toom toom toom* that chanted throughout my childhood and adolescence was replaced by the melody of my grandmother's words that invoke my ancestors: they were the sound that accompanied me when I returned to my old world, in which I had no real place, in which my voice was not heard.

I had to reinvent it for me, thanks to music, thanks to dancing.

It took a lot of changes.

Federico and I split up. We've taken different paths because both of us need to reclaim our own lives, our own roots, and our own hidden treasures. Both of us had flourishing branches and trees to nourish. Maybe one day each of us will be able to travel lighter. The important thing is not to stop, to never stop searching.

When I came back from Liberia, I brought an indescribable energy with me that pushed me to continue the search for belonging, that no longer had the same urgency as before but that was driven by a greater awareness.

For a while, I continued to find the fact of not being officially Italian unbearable. I felt I could no longer go around recognized only by a digital code, forever waiting to have a residence permit or citizenship.

For years I was a case number, but that number wasn't me, even though I couldn't help but identify with it. But then I let myself be fueled by renewed energy. I strengthened myself by overcoming every bureaucratic obstacle. I achieved citizenship and this piece too, little by little, fell into place.

And my body too, by now, has taken another form: my body is present, my body moves in streets that belong to it. My body is no longer a barrier: my body is African, it is Italian, my body is.

It was Africa that made me understand that I also belong to Italy, that I can be everything, that I don't have borders, because my body no longer has limits.

It's only my body.

The Black body.

My body is flesh.

My body is beautiful because it's Black.

My body is a temple.

My body moves and speaks without taboos.

My body is a metaphor; it communicates and allows itself to be interpreted.

My body is nature.

My body has a color and in the streets they point it out to me.

I feel my body reborn.

I feel my body resurface.

My body has a soul, just longing to talk.

I live in this body; I can leave and come back as I please.

If I look at it from the outside, I see how you want to look at it.

If I look at it from the inside, I hurt myself.

I live in my body, I nourish it, I admire it.

And I don't let it dominate me.

I choose to live in my Black body.

Notes on Contributors

ANNA MARIA GEHNYEI, also known as Karima 2G, is a singer, rapper, dancer, beatsmith, and producer born in Rome to Liberian parents. *The Black Body*, her first book, delves into her experience growing up as a second-generation Black Italian.

EILIS KIERANS is assistant professor of teaching in the Italian department at the Pennsylvania State University. She is the coeditor of the translation series Other Voices of Italy. She has published articles on the work of Gabriella Kuruvilla, Grazia Deledda, Dacia Maraini, lesbian Italian American writers, and Christian Petzold.

SANDRA WATERS is the managing editor of *Italian Quarterly* and coedits the Other Voices of Italy series. Her recent publications include chapters and articles on Luther Blissett and Wu Ming, Paolo Sorrentino, and American horror film. She edited *The Spaces and Places of Horror* and cotranslated Porpora Marcasciano's *AntoloGaia* for OVOI.

IGIABA SCEGO is a Somali Italian writer, cultural activist, and freelance scholar. She was born in Rome to Somali parents who took refuge in Italy following a coup d'état in their native country, where her father served as foreign minister.

She holds a PhD in education on postcolonial subjects, has done extensive academic work in Italy and around the world, and has a special interest in immigration and mobility. Her first memoir won Italy's prestigious Mondello Prize. Her novel *The Color Line* won the Premio Napoli. Scego received the International Viareggio-Répaci award in 2021. Most recently, she was longlisted for the Premio Strega for her second memoir, *Cassandra a Mogadiscio.* Her previous novels include *Beyond Babylon* and *Adua.* She also coedited the anthology series Africana (Feltrinelli) with Chiara Piaggio.

Titles in the **Other Voices of Italy** series:

Carmine Abate, *The Round Dance*. Translated by Michelangelo La Luna

Giuseppe Berto, *Glory: The Gospel of Judas, A Novel*. Translated by Gregory Conti

Giuseppe Berto, *Oh, Serafina!* Translated by Gregory Conti

Adrián Bravi, *My Language Is a Jealous Lover*. Translated by Victoria Offredi Poletto and Giovanna Bellesia Contuzzi

Angelo Cannavacciuolo, *When Things Happen*. Translated by Gregory Pell

Shirin Ramzanali Fazel and Simone Brioni, *Islam and Me: Narrating a Diaspora*. Translated by Shirin Ramzanali Fazel and Simone Brioni

Anna Maria Gehnyei, *The Black Body*. Translated by Eilis Kierans and Sandra Waters

Alessandro Giardino, *The Caravaggio Syndrome*. Translated by Joyce Meyerson with Alessandro Giardino

Ugo Boncompagni Ludovisi, *The Twilight of Rome's Papal Nobility: The Life of Agnese Borghese Boncompagni Ludovisi*. Translated by Carol Cofone

Geneviève Makaping, *Reversing the Gaze: What If the Other Were You?* Translated by Giovanna Bellesia Contuzzi and Victoria Offredi Poletto

Dacia Maraini, *In Praise of Disobedience: Clare of Assisi*. Translated by Jane Tylus

Dacia Maraini, *Life, Brazen and Garish*. Translated by Elvira DiFabio

Porpora Marcasciano, *AntoloGaia: Queering the Seventies, A Radical Trans Memoir*. Translated by Francesco Pascuzzi and Sandra Waters

Luigi Pirandello, *The Outcast*. Translated by Bradford A. Masoni